The Which? Guide to
Self-Catering Holidays Abroad

The Which? Guide to
Self-Catering
Holidays Abroad

Roger Macdonald

Published by Consumers' Association
and Hodder & Stoughton

Which? Books are commissioned and researched by
The Association for Consumer Research
and published by Consumers' Association,
2 Marylebone Road, London NW1 4DX, and
Hodder & Stoughton, 47 Bedford Square,
London WC1B 3DP

Typographic design by Tim Higgins
Cover artwork by Ray Evans
Maps by Eugene Fleury

First edition 1990

British Library Cataloguing in Publication Data
Macdonald, Roger
    The Which? guide to self-catering holidays abroad.
    1. Europe. Self-catering accommodation
    I. Title II. Consumers' Association III. Series
    647.94

ISBN 0 340 49198 1

Typeset in Linotron Meridien
by Litho Link Ltd, Welshpool, Powys
Printed and bound in Great Britain by
BPCC Hazell Books
Aylesbury, Bucks, England
Member of BPCC Ltd.

Contents

Introduction

For some people, self-catering holidays on the Continent conjure up an image of housework transferred, of an unpredictable cooker and washing-up liquid with a foreign label. But this is by no means the whole story, or, indeed, a typical one. You can now find self-catering accommodation with ultra-modern equipment, sometimes including a dishwasher, and many places offer not only a maid who cleans and makes the beds, but even a cook.

Many self-catering holiday-makers in any case eat most of their meals at restaurants – when they and their families feel hungry, rather than at some hotel's set meal-times, and in friendly, inexpensive little restaurants that positively welcome rather than tolerate children.

Self-catering also means that you do not have to rely on finding a hotel with room service to provide a late-night bottle of warm milk for the baby, who wants it within sixty seconds, not when it suits the hotels taff.

For couples without children, self-catering can be the ideal spontaneous holiday, with accommodation booked at the last minute or even arranged on the spot.

And self-catering means that you can come and go as you please. You can stay up as late as you like, make as much noise as you like (within reason), and sleep until lunchtime without upsetting the chambermaid's routine.

Of course, there are snags. A self-catering holiday is not necessarily a rest cure. It can be more expensive than a down-market hotel package tour. Things sometimes taken for granted, such as transport from the airport to your accommodation, can be expensive and difficult to organise. Entertainment may be scarce, and families can become bored with their own company. Lifelong friends sometimes discover that they are incompatible when they share a house. Self-catering can require a lot of personal initiative when things to wrong.

This guide cannot guarantee a good self-catering

holiday, but it will reduce the risk of failure. Each of the five most popular self-catering countries – France, Greece, Italy, Portugal and Spain – is diagnosed in detail: how to get there; what weather to expect; the kind of properties available; shopping for food; eating out; local transport; what to take with you and what to bring back. Every significant resort in the main tourist regions has been visited in order to assess what it has to offer the self-catering holiday-maker: its accommodation, its beaches, its attractions, its ambience and any drawbacks.

The book also tries to ensure that holiday-makers have the widest possible choice of property to consider. It lists practically every organisation that offers self-catering accommodation in the most popular holiday areas. Having decided on which country you want to go to, you should find the most suitable-sounding location in the chapter on that country, then consult the list of tour operators that offer self-catering accommodation there. Full details of each operator are given in the separate chapter on tour operators; each entry specifies in which region, or on what island, the operator offers self-catering properties. You can then consider all the options by obtaining details of properties from the brochures of all the relevant tour operators.

Successful self-catering holidays require a little homework before you make a choice. This book suggests the questions you should ask to ensure that you get the holiday you expect – not unpleasant surprises.

France

France does not feature prominently among the self-catering holidays in the brochures of major UK tour operators. The unbending opposition of the French aviation authority to charter flights on any significant scale makes package holiday-makers mainly reliant on scheduled flights, which are too expensive for the mass market. Those inclusive arrangements that do exist predominantly involve cross-Channel ferries and/or Motorail, with the customer taking his or her own car.

The field is largely left clear for smaller operators and independent companies, many of them choosing not to sell through established travel agents but instead to market their holidays direct. As their products may consist solely of self-catering accommodation, or at any rate not fall within the accepted definition of an inclusive tour, such organisations may not be required to deposit the bond that serves as a protection for the holiday-maker should the company run into financial difficulties. By buying direct, their clients often benefit in price but at the expense of the separate protection provided by the Association of British Travel Agents (ABTA) for holidays booked through their members. Most small companies are properly run; but for added security holiday-makers would be well advised to use a credit card to finance their booking, as the credit card company would be liable to reimburse them if the travel company went out of business.

France is the land of the *gîte*. The strict definition of a *gîte* is a lodging-house or dwelling of any kind, which allows holiday companies to use the term as a marketing device to promote almost any type of property to let. However, the *gîte* has its origins in the government-controlled system introduced in 1955, which gave loans and tax concessions to owners of run-down country property provided that the owners undertook to let the property as holiday homes for at least ten years.

The organisation that began as a kind of fiscal police force to stop owners getting improvement loans under false pretences – the *Fédération Nationale des Gîtes de France* – is now a huge booking agency with offices in every French *département*. It deals with what are known as *gîtes ruraux*, privately owned holiday homes in the French countryside. They may be individual cottages or self-contained parts of an existing dwelling, but in each case they have to fulfil these minimum requirements:

- own lockable front door,
- flushable toilet with modern seat,
- bathroom with shower,
- facility for cooking and (possible extra charge) for heating shower water,
- cooking equipment and utensils,
- refrigerator, and
- shutters and curtains.

The cooker and water heater usually work on a bottled gas cylinder. The price of the *gîte* may include one such cylinder, but visitors are often expected to pay for and fit any replacement. Heating will either be electric or consist of a traditional oil stove (*poêle*) that uses a fuel called *mazout*. The latter can be tricky to use, so make sure you get a thorough demonstration.

Each *gîte rural* is awarded between one and three *épis* (ears of corn). Those *gîtes* in the highest category are expected either to be 'comfortable and well furnished' or to be located in an area of 'outstanding natural interest or recreational opportunity'. It must be said, however, that many *gîtes* have decidedly uncomfortable beds, practically no easy chairs, and facilities bordering on the spartan. Most are cheap and excellent value for money but they are not the rural equivalent of a well-equipped villa in the South of France.

If you wish to book a *gîte* through official channels in the UK, you must first become a member of the Gîtes de France Club (178 Piccadilly, London W1V 9DB; telephone 071-493 3480 between 9 a.m. and 5.30 p.m. Monday to Saturday). For a small fee the club will send you a brochure containing more than 2000 *gîtes*, which are reserved for peak-period British bookings until the end of May in any given year. Thereafter, Gîtes de France have to check the availability of a particular *gîte* with their appropriate French office.

The *gîtes* marketed by travel companies, particularly ferry operators, are usually reserved for their own clients until two weeks before any given booking date. Only then will they be released back to the owners to see if they can rent their *gîte* through other channels. In some instances these *gîtes* are more up-market than the basic product. They include, for example, restored country houses, which are significantly more expensive than the average *gîte*.

Local agencies (called *Services Loisirs Accueil*) run by local authorities throughout France may also have properties on their books outside the normal range of *gîtes*. They can be contacted via the local Tourist Information Office (*Syndicat d'Initiative*), whose addresses and telephone numbers are printed in the *Guide Michelin* hotel and restaurant guide.

In all, more than 30,000 *gîtes ruraux* are available to rent in France. For a full list in a particular region, write to the local *gîte* office (called *Relais Départementaux*) or to the local town hall. The French National Tourist Office (178 Piccadilly, London W1V 0AL; telephone 071-491 7622 between 9 a.m. and 5 p.m. Monday to Saturday; start dialling before 9 to beat the rush) can provide most of the appropriate regional addresses. However, any literature sent to you from France will be entirely in French, and most offices will expect you to make the actual booking direct with the owner, whose knowledge of English may be limited.

11

The effort could prove worthwhile, nevertheless, as many of the most agreeable *gîtes* never reach the British market; sometimes because the local owner cannot be bothered with foreign tourists, but more often because they are easily let and always in use during July and August.

The French holiday season remains the most inflexible in Europe, with virtually the entire population taking leave in this period, and *gîtes* fully occupied. For the rest of the year, booking a hotel in the region of your choice for one or two nights should be sufficient time for you to find a vacant *gîte* after your arrival, when you have all the advantage of seeing the property for yourself and negotiating a price on the spot, against a background where the owner had not been expecting to make anything in the coming week or fortnight. Even families with children can embark on this slightly adventurous approach without real fear of a disaster.

In sharp contrast to *gîtes*, in popular tourist areas, particularly in Mediterranean and ski resorts, purpose-built apartment blocks are common. Most have lifts and all amenities, and the high-season rental price reflects the fact that demand often exceeds supply.

Provence and the Côte d'Azur also specialise in the truly luxurious villa, with private swimming-pool, bedrooms with en suite and lavishly equipped bathrooms, and impeccable furnishings. Because their owners (and agents) have a morbid fear of the house being ruined by some undesirable visitors, or the telephone being used for innumerable international calls, they invariably require a huge deposit, known as a *caution*. Any breakages or unexpected costs are simply deducted from this deposit and the tenants refunded the balance – though sometimes after a considerable delay. The grandest houses also come with a compulsory staff, including a maid, gardener and cook, whose wages form part of the weekly rent. Even sharing such a house with several friends may still leave you to find a sum of money more usually associated with full board at a luxury hotel.

Many such properties are handled locally by estate

agents (*agents immobiliers*), who have the principal contract with the owners. Where the property also appears in a holiday brochure, therefore, it will often be at a premium, as the local estate agent will expect his commission out of the proceeds. Some particularly luxurious villas may go through several tiers of nominal supervision, each agent successively claiming a commission, with the result that a brochure price will be hugely inflated. Fortunately, the best British companies marketing French self-catering accommodation deal direct with the owners of properties. Ask for written assurance that this applies to the property of your choice, to be sure of paying a realistic price for your holiday.

France has the greatest range, and the greatest number, of self-catering properties in Europe. No one knows exactly how many: for each one let officially through a company or an organisation, another is probably let by word of mouth through friends of friends. Most of the real owners of holiday homes, however affluent, seem to take a delight in escaping the clutches of the French equivalent of the Inland Revenue. Even the most reputable of British companies offering French properties to rent are under intense pressure from some owners to pay them in cash.

There are therefore more opportunities in France than elsewhere to eliminate the middleman. A few enterprising British holiday-makers comb their villa for evidence of the address of the owner of the property, such as a gas bill, with the intention of booking with him direct the following year. No doubt this can work, and can save a good deal of money, but the risks are considerable.

First, French owners, as already said, prefer to be paid in cash, and that will include the deposit. However, they also forget, or sometimes disregard, exactly when they have rented out their property. Stories abound of British holiday-makers, booked direct with owners, who find themselves double-booked or descended upon in mid-holiday by friends of the owner 'promised' the property for the weekend or longer.

Secondly, French owners are reluctant to spend much money on holiday homes. Items that may be essential to the success of a family self-catering holiday, such as a cooker or washing machine, are sometimes left unrepaired. A vigilant holiday company is able to avert many such disasters.

Thirdly, French holiday homes are invariably looked after by local caretakers. The effort they make in basic maintenance, watering the garden and, especially, in keeping the swimming-pool clean and tidy is often in direct proportion to the strength of the lines of communication to the owner. A British family that has been given access to the property on the cheap by a cash deal direct with the owner is likely to exert rather less influence than a holiday company with a permanent representative in the area and a contract for the season.

What to take with you

Unless you are flying to the South of France, a self-catering holiday in France is usually more convenient by car, and allows much greater flexibility in terms of luggage. Even if you have booked a luxury villa, it is surprising how many items that you take for granted in the UK may not be instantly available.

In some accommodation, bed linen is not provided, although blankets will be. Check exactly the type and size of beds to be sure of taking the correct combination of sheets. The French rest their heads on bolsters, a hard device tucked under the bottom sheet and designed to give most foreign visitors a crick in the neck. French pillows are invariably square, and defy all attempts to fit them inside British pillow cases. The only solution, if this is something that bothers you, is to take enough pillows and pillow cases from home to dispense with the French versions altogether.

The French prescribe tea for convalescent patients, and do not take it seriously as a standard drink. Do not expect to find a teapot, a kettle or an economic supply of quality teabags in France: take them with you, together with an adaptor or a Continental plug for the kettle. Instant coffee is more expensive in most parts of France.

The French do not eat boiled eggs for breakfast, so assume that your self-catering holiday home will not have egg-cups.

If you are staying in the countryside, assume the worst and take with you those items whose unexpected absence will cause you inconvenience. These include a bottle-opener and tin-opener, a corkscrew, matches, candles (short power cuts are common in the countryside), soap, coat-hangers, tea-towels, cleaning materials, refuse bags and a sharp kitchen knife.

Also recommended is a pair of pliers for emergency repairs, a small adjustable spanner for connecting cooking-gas bottles, a torch with new batteries and a set of small screwdrivers.

There are also certain categories of food which are either difficult to find or expensive. They include ketchup, Marmite, peanut butter, pickles, Heinz baked beans, cornflakes and chunky marmalade.

Eating in

In contrast to those in the UK, small shops in France, far from being in decline, are actually increasing in number. In a country where quality and service are still very much appreciated, the small man survives, sometimes at great personal inconvenience. Take, for example, *la boulangerie*, the baker's shop. The baker may be up at 3.30 a.m. every morning, including Sundays, and, apart from a few hours' rest in the afternoons, still be working at 7 or 8 p.m. As well as *baguettes* (literally, 'wands'), the archetypal long French loaves, and *le pain de campagne*, a huge round rustic-looking loaf, the baker sells *croissants* and, very popular with children, *pain au chocolat*, a kind of *croissant* with chocolate in the centre.

Like the baker's, most food shops open their doors at 8 a.m. or earlier and close surprisingly promptly at midday to reopen at around 3 p.m., even later in the hottest parts of the South of France. They stay open until at least 7 p.m. and sometimes as late as 8.30. On Sundays they may open a little later, and you would be very fortunate to find a food shop open anywhere after midday. On Mondays, to compensate for an otherwise gruelling week, they may be closed during the morning and sometimes all day. But you will usually find that one shop corners the local trade by staying open on Monday and closing on another midweek day instead.

The baker's may also be a cake-shop, a *pâtisserie*, which in larger towns will be a separate shop altogether. Either way, it will produce on the premises a large variety of breathtaking (in taste and price) gâteaux, fresh fruit tarts and delicious éclairs.

A French grocer's (*l'épicerie*) often takes on a very wide brief, and can be a large shop that may well be part dairy, part traditional greengrocer's, selling fruit and vegetables, and part off-licence. Most French shoppers go here to buy milk. They usually prefer the long-life variety, although fresh milk is available, graded into red top (full cream), blue top (skimmed or semi-skimmed) and green top (fat-free).

L'alimentation générale, the general store, can be both baffling and frustrating for British visitors, as no two seem to stock the same goods. However, nearly all of them have crisps, biscuits and tinned food (much less popular in France than in the UK), and some sell fruit, vegetables and various dairy products.

The dairy (*crémerie*) is a specialised store selling butter, cheese, milk, cream and other dairy-related items. Butter is taken as seriously as wine (it is even *appellation contrôlée*) in France and no self-respecting Frenchman buys margarine (which is never coloured yellow). Normandy and Brittany specialise in unsalted butter.

Cheese shops (*fromageries*) are nowadays found only in major towns, as cheese is sold in many different shops. In all, 246 varieties of cheese are available in France, divided into four major categories. They are blue (Roquefort, for example), cream (Boursin, for example), soft (Brie or Camembert), and hard (Emmental, for example).

Greengrocers (*marchands de légumes*) are relatively rare outside large towns, although you may see signs for a *fruitier* (fruit shop) or for a *primeur*, someone who sells early crops of choice fruit and vegetables. All these, however, are generally superfluous because of the market (*marché*), which often consists of a convoy of trailers which may well move from town to town on different market days. France has an abundant supply of home-grown produce, superior to and cheaper than the equivalent in the UK. Although most prices are marked per kilo, French shoppers pick out the exact items they want, put them in one of the containers provided, and leave the stallholder to weigh and price them. Markets open before 8 a.m. and gradually close up after midday.

French butchers (*boucheries*) offer better value than their British equivalent, because most meat is sold free of major bones and excess fat, and what is weighed is often entirely edible. The butcher also slices the meat in a different way: he does not provide 'joints' but 'cuts', sliced along the muscles rather than across them. The best cuts are *filet, contre-filet, entrecôte, rumsteck* and *faux-filet*. If you are making hamburgers, ask for *bifteck haché*, fat-free minced beef. Lamb chops are *côtes* or *côtelettes d'agneau*, and a leg of lamb is a *gigot*. Under French law only a *boucherie chevaline* is permitted to sell horsemeat, and the shop has a clearly identifiable red or gold representation of a horse's head above the doorway. Although horsemeat tastes and costs much the same as beef, few British visitors can be persuaded to try it. The standard butcher sells proper beef, lamb, mutton, veal and sometimes fresh game (of which *la pintade*, guinea-fowl, is a French favourite) and poultry (*volaille*). Birds usually come with head, feet and innards still intact. A free-range chicken, *un poulet fermier*, costs nearly twice as much, but may be worth the extra. The butcher rarely sells pork, unless he is a *boucherie-charcuterie*. The *charcuterie* is strictly a pork butcher's, the word deriving from *chair cuite* (cooked meat). *Chair* (meaning 'flesh') still exists as a kind of raw sausagemeat, decidedly an acquired taste. Depending on the skill of the proprietor, this shop has become an ambitious delicatessen, offering a wide range of pâtés, pies, pizzas, quiches and salads – in fact all kinds of ready-prepared dishes (sometimes sold in a separate shop, *le traiteur*).

Except in large towns, fishmongers (*poissonneries*) have

been largely superseded by market stalls (especially in ports, of course) and supermarkets. The French distribution system succeeds in providing fresh fish daily, however far from the sea. Monkfish (*lotte*), sole, turbot and whiting (*merlan*) are usually good value. The fishmonger will clean (*vider*) and fillet (*découper en filets*) the fish if you ask him to.

Wine merchants are much less common than they used to be, their trade taken by grocers and supermarkets, which are much more competitive in price. Middle-range-priced wines will cost half to two-thirds of the cost of a similar bottle bought in the UK, so could be worth bringing back within your duty-free allowance. These include good-quality Bordeaux, Beaujolais and Muscadet, Sancerre, Chablis and Pouilly-Fuissé.

Just about every enterprising grocer who operates on a self-service principle describes his shop as a *supermarché*, so for serious large-scale shopping find a hypermarket (*hypermarché*), officially defined as a supermarket with more than 2500 square metres of selling space. There are at least 350 of these huge shops throughout France, selling a great range of goods as well as food. This is convenience shopping in every sense: for example, its poultry is marked PAC (short for *prêt-à-cuire*, oven-ready). Most hypermarkets have large car-parks, sometimes with petrol at discount prices. Most are open from 9 a.m. to 10 p.m. Monday to Saturday, but, apart from the cafeteria, few open on Sundays. Some take credit cards, or even sterling, though the rate of exchange is not particularly favourable.

Eating out

French restaurants differ from those in the UK in three important aspects. First, they are not full of people who dislike children. Secondly, the majority of them will never expect you to hurry your meal. Thirdly, a much broader stratum of French society regularly eats out, helped by the fact that the cost of a restaurant meal represents in real terms a much smaller part of their disposable income. The result generally is a more relaxed environment than in

British restaurants, with many more family-run, well-patronised restaurants offering a high standard of cuisine at prices most British visitors will find eminently reasonable.

By law, every French restaurant (although a few in out-of-the-way places do not) has to display its menus outside, so that you can see the cost of each item in advance. The shorter the menu, the better the chance that the food will be personally prepared. Restaurants must also offer at least one fixed-price menu, including service and taxes (though coffee is always extra). This will often prove the best value for money, but avoid in holiday areas the *menu touristique*, which often consists of cheap dishes for the uncomplaining tourist. At the other end of the scale, order the *menu gastronomique* only if your appetite is as large as your pocket.

Allow plenty of time. In France, ordering a meal is an art form in itself, not to be rushed. Do not be afraid to ask if you are unsure about a particular dish. Remember that in France meat is traditionally under-cooked. If, for example, you want the equivalent of 'medium' in the UK, ask for '*bien cuit*', literally 'well done'. '*A point*' is the equivalent of British 'rare'; '*bleu*' indicates that it has scarcely touched the pan.

Restaurants serve meals at set hours, usually 12.30–3 and around 7.30–10, closing earlier in the countryside, later in major towns. If you want a meal between those hours, find a brasserie, which will serve a single dish or more throughout the day. '*La brasserie*' originally meant simply a brewery, so it may be presumed that alcohol, rather than food, was once its priority; this is no longer the case. The French are not enthusiasts for snacks, but most cafés offer a *croque-monsieur*, a delicious toasted sandwich with a mixture of cheese and ham.

At the height of the season it is often essential to book a restaurant table. This also applies throughout the year to Sunday lunch, the most popular family meal. Avoid restaurants on Sunday and Monday evenings, because even if they are open it may well be the chef's two evenings off.

Children

Children are enthusiastically welcomed, rather than simply tolerated, in all parts of France – especially in restaurants. This is good news if you have children, possibly rather less so if you do not. It should be mentioned that French children are introduced to restaurants at a very young age, and tend to take such occasions in their stride; they are often given wine, diluted with mineral water, almost as soon as they can hold a glass.

Many *gîtes* are on farm property, and care needs to be taken to ensure that children stay well out of the way of farm machinery, which can be dangerous.

Although cots are provided on request in the majority of self-catering accommodation, a really secure cot with high sides is comparatively rare, as French children are moved into proper beds at an early age. If you have a child aged over two accustomed only to sleeping in a cot, take a travel cot.

Transport

Tolls are charged on all French motorways; payment may be made in cash or by credit card. The police make random checks on the time stamps on motorway entry cards to see if motorists have driven the distance above the speed-limit. There are heavy fines for speeding and other minor traffic offences, which must be paid in cash. Speed-limits are lower in wet weather, defined as any occasion when a driver has to use his windscreen wipers.

Motorways and major roads suffer from severe congestion and multiple accidents during the French holiday season, July and August. Alternative routes (*itinéraire bis*), marked by yellow signs with black lettering and the word *bis* in a circle, avoid major conurbations and, though slower, are much more agreeable.

Cars may be hired in all major French towns and cities and can be expected to be in good working order. French Railways (SNCF) offer discounted rates for car hire from more than 2000 railway stations.

On all except international trains, travellers are expected to date-stamp (*composter*) their tickets, using the machine at the entrance to the platform. Failure to do so can result in a fine of up to 20 per cent of the full value of the ticket.

Partly because of the excellence of French trains, few bus services operate over long distances (other than those starting in the UK). Rural bus services, unable to compete with a subsidised railway, are practically non-existent, although a few buses run between villages on market days.

Avoiding problems

The chemist's shop (*pharmacie*) is operated on a personal basis in France; there are no chains. The pharmacist is therefore individually responsible for all prescriptions and advice, and is particularly well qualified. However, although he has at his disposal a number of powerful drugs, in France, as in the UK, he will be reluctant to hand them out without a doctor's prescription. He will be well placed to know the whereabouts of the nearest doctor.

For most medical problems, consult a GP, *un généraliste*. He will be quite happy to make a personal visit, as he can charge more. Assuming that you have taken out proper medical insurance, this will not present you with any difficulty in recovering his fee and the cost of his prescription. It is possible to recover 75 per cent of medical charges through reciprocal EC arrangements via form E111, but if you have taken out personal travel insurance there is no incentive to do so.

For real emergencies: police, dial 17; fire, dial 18. Ambulance services are regional, usually with the first two figures common to all local numbers, then 67 00 00.

Opening hours

Most food shops generally open from 8 a.m. to noon and from 3 to 7 p.m. (or even later) from Tuesday to Saturday. On Sunday they open from 8 a.m. to 11.30; they may close all or part of Monday.

Other shops generally open from 9.30 to noon and from 3 to 7 p.m. Monday to Saturday. Department stores open from 9.30 a.m. to 6 p.m. Monday to Saturday. Most hypermarkets and large supermarkets open from 9 a.m. to 10 p.m. Monday to Saturday.

Banking hours vary from region to region, but the most common opening times are 9 a.m. to noon and 2 to 4.30 p.m. Monday to Friday. In some towns, especially those with a Saturday market, the banks may open on Saturday and close instead on Monday. They are also closed on Sundays and every Bank Holiday.

Public holidays

1 January (New Year's Day); **Easter Monday; 1 May** (Labour Day); **8 May** (VE Day); **the sixth Thursday after Easter** (Ascension Day); **the second Monday after Ascension Day** (Whit Monday); **14 July** (Bastille Day); **15 August** (the Feast of The Assumption of the Virgin Mary); **1 November** (*Toussaint*, All Saints' Day); **11 November** (Armistice Day); **25 December** (Christmas Day)

What to bring back

Middle-range-priced wines
Liqueurs
Cognac
French beer
Wine vinegar
Cheese
Garlic
Quality tinned soups
Mustard
Pâté de foie gras
Toys
Bicycles
Track shoes
Car tyres (from hypermarkets)
Barbecues in kit form
Power tools
Casserole dishes
Kitchen gadgets
Crystal glass
Household linen
Ski equipment
Stationery

Tour operators

For details see page 213

Agence France Holidays
Allez France
Andrews, Peter
Angel Travel
Avon Europe
BCH Villa France
Beach Villas
Belvedere Holiday Apartments
Blakes Holidays
Bowhill Holidays
Brimar International
Brittany Direct Holidays
Brittany Ferries
Chalets de France
Chapter Travel
Chez Nous
Clearwater Holidays
Coast & Country Villas
Continental Villas
Cordon Rouge Villas
Cresta Holidays
Crystal Holiday
CV Travel
Destination Provence

Dominique's Villas
Drive Europe
Euro Express
European Villas
Eurovillas
Exclusive Villas
Four Seasons
La France des Villages
France Directe
France Voyages
French Affair
French Country Cottages
French Life
French Travel Service
French Villa Centre
Gîtes de France
GMF Holidays
Harry Shaw Holidays
Harvey's à la Carte
Headwater Holidays
Hoseasons Holidays
    Abroad
Images of France
Interhome
International Chapters
Jafa Holidays
Kingsland Holidays
Meon Travel
Miraleisure
Miss France Holidays
NAT Holidays
Newman, David

NSS Riviera Holidays
P & O European Ferries
Palm Luxury Villas
Palmer & Parker Holidays
PDO Holidays
Pleasurewood Holidays
La Première Quality Villas
Prime Time Holidays
Les Propriétaires de l'Ouest
Quo Vadis
Redwing Holidays
Rendezvous France
RentaVilla
Sally Holidays
Savoir-Faire
SBH France
Sealink Holidays
SFV Holidays
Slipaway Holidays
Starvillas
Sturge, Martin
Sunscene Holidays
Sunselect Villas
Sunvista Holidays
Vacances
Vacances en Campagne
Vacances France
VFB Holidays
The Villa Agency
The Villa Collection
Villa France

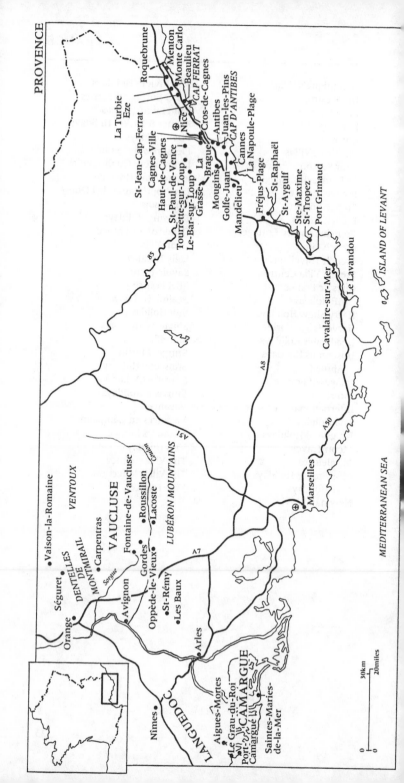

Provence and the Côte d'Azur

Provence is the epicentre of the truly rewarding self-catering holiday. Wherever you choose to stay, however grand or humble, it will offer one or more of the marvellous attractions of the South of France: a chance to see the great monuments left behind by the Romans in Provincia – literally, 'the province' – at Nîmes, Arles and Orange and the Pont-du-Gard aqueduct, and the palaces that mark the age when Avignon displaced Rome as the residence of the Pope; a chance to absorb the intoxicating pleasures of the Riviera, still the playground of the rich and famous; a chance to suspend time itself in the rocky retreats and countryside of inland Provence, where man and machine seem to have been undisturbed for centuries.

It may be difficult to imagine it now, but in the early 1920s only one hotel remained open in Menton during the summer, and there were so few visitors to Antibes in August that the local telephone switchboard closed down altogether in the evenings. But not for long. The invention of insecticides (keeping down the mosquitoes), the availability of fridges and sun cream sustained a relentless momentum towards summer holidays on the Riviera, initiated by the Americans, who disliked crossing the Atlantic in rough weather. The Americans called the tune because they alone had the money: the European aristocracy had been decimated or bankrupted by the Great War, and had left the South of France, most never to return. The days when the Riviera was a refuge for British invalids or the wealthy seeking to escape harsh winters were an even more distant memory.

Menton is still something of a health resort, with little nightlife and most holiday-makers staying in expensive hotels by the sea. However, for the determined visitor, there is self-catering accommodation available in the old quarter, among the stepped alleyways and seventeenth-century Italianate houses.

You would have to pay a great deal more to stay in a flat in **Monte Carlo**, in the independent principality of

Monaco, although the majority of apartments have a view of the millionaires' yachts in the harbour. Much of the accommodation is owned by companies whose executives are elsewhere during July and August, so one tip is to scan the personal columns of the Riviera's most-read newspaper, *Nice-Matin*, where such flats may be let cheaply to anyone with impeccable references.

Even grander – too grand for most people's pockets – are the villas back in France itself with a view at **Beaulieu**, a rather languid if sophisticated resort, and on the peninsula of **Cap Ferrat**, full of millionaires jealous of their privacy. For those who like to give a misleading impression of their holiday arrangements, somewhat poky but much cheaper apartments exist in the adjacent tiny port of **St-Jean-Cap-Ferrat**, close to the marina.

Nice itself has many apartments to rent, but beware of staying too close to the famous Promenade des Anglais, which is a little like Brands Hatch during Grand Prix practice. You have to pay to go on most of the beaches, which are pebble. Their seaside restaurants offer high quality but expensive cuisine. The best flats are near the rue Massena, in an area that has been turned into a pedestrian zone, with outdoor cafés.

More modest houses may be rented behind the Riviera proper, near the hillside villages of **Roquebrune, Eze** and **La Turbie**, though staying in Eze can be spoilt by the huge influx of coach-tours.

East of Nice is a resort to be avoided at all costs, **Cros-de-Cagnes**, with a unique combination of urbanised motorways, high-rise apartments and congested supermarkets. Immediately behind it, **Cagnes-Ville** is equally commercial and extremely noisy. Only **Haut-de-Cagnes**, a good way from the sea, offers agreeable surroundings, but it has little to suit the self-catering holiday-maker.

Again, the little inland towns, perched high in the foothills of the Alpes-Maritimes, offer much better value, especially **St-Paul-de-Vence**, and two overlooking the spectacular Gorges de Loup, **Le-Bar-sur-Loup** and **Tourrette-sur-Loup**. Further west, **Grasse**, of perfume fame, has reasonably priced apartments and a kind of innocuous charm, but the town lacks both the calm of the countryside and the glitter of the Mediterranean resorts.

As the coastline swings south, the culture shock of Cros-de-Cagnes is scarcely diluted by the brash **La Brague**, where much new development is taking place. Many holiday flats are within easy walking distance of the inappropriately named Siesta Club, a dynamic lido by day, a *son-et-lumière* disco by night. It is the ideal place for bored teenagers, and parents can leave younger children in a supervised adventure playground.

Antibes offers some beautiful apartments overlooking the marina, but the rental price goes up floor by floor. South of Antibes, the true affluence of the Riviera is in evidence on the peninsula of **Cap d'Antibes**, full of luxurious holiday apartments and even more luxurious villas. In sharp contrast, **Juan-les-Pins**, which has much cheaper accommodation, is full of young and unsophisticated visitors with plenty of energy but few resources. The beaches in this area are sandy and greatly overcrowded in mid-summer; in winter the place is virtually deserted. Weekend crowds can be overwhelming at **Golfe-Juan**, an undistinguished resort notable only for the fact that, unlike the rest of the Riviera, most of its beaches are free.

In the hills behind Cannes, villas cluster around **Mougins**, a fashionable evening eating-place. Non-golfers should note that the much-admired local golf course puts a premium on rented houses within walking distance of it.

Cannes itself has very little self-catering accommodation, and much of what is available is small and shabby. The town is best avoided during the Film Festival each May, when the prices go up sharply and every restaurant is crowded. Cannes' beaches of imported sand are expensive, but there is a surprisingly agreeable public beach at the east end of the town, close to the children's playground.

Inland, east of Cannes, **Mandelieu** is the nondescript villa administration centre for much of the Riviera. Several local representatives of tour companies reside here in summer, and many local rental agencies have offices. Despite its good connections, as a place at which to stay it leaves much to be desired. Its coastal suburb, **La Napoule-Plage**, has a sandy beach and some pleasant but expensive apartments.

The coast road runs south-east to **St-Raphaël**, which has strong claims to be the oldest self-catering centre in recorded history. Wealthy Ancient Roman families built villas here, on the site of the modern casino, complete with sun terraces overlooking the sea, and came regularly for their summer holidays. St-Raphaël remains a family resort, with modest prices and a particularly safe sandy beach sloping gently into the sea. The nightlife is only marginally more obtrusive than that of Eastbourne or Tunbridge Wells.

Further east, there are many apartments to rent close to **Fréjus-Plage**, but visitors who stay here should have no illusions. The Benidorm of the Riviera, Fréjus-Plage is brash, ugly and noisy. In summer thousands of visitors, including many young people, are crammed like penned sheep into a long, narrow strip of sand between the sea and a coast road with continuous traffic from dawn to dusk.

St-Aygulf has a number of fashionable villas in an otherwise unfashionable resort. Many of its restaurants are cheap, cheerful, and good value, reflecting the fact that the majority of its visitors are on a tight budget. The sandy beach is very similar to the English South Coast, mainly hard, slightly damp sand.

Ste-Maxime works much harder to keep its visitors amused, with fêtes and fairs throughout the summer, a thriving casino and five nightclubs. Its sandy beach, south facing, becomes extremely crowded during high season. Most self-catering is at the back of the town, a brisk walk from the promenade. Restaurants are over-priced, but the town's daily vegetable market provides a wide range of cheap local produce.

Continuing south-east, **Port Grimaud** is the major self-catering centre of the Riviera, fashionable and expensive. Modelled on a medieval fishing port by its architect,

François Spoerry, it consists of a network of artificial canals and mock-Venetian bridges clustered around a central lagoon. The majority of the houses, of two or three floors, extremely narrow, with little gardens fronting on to the canals, are rented out by local agencies. The most attractive overlook the harbour entrance, where you can watch the millionaires' yachts sail past, like a line of graceful swans, or back on to the sandy beach, which is relatively inaccessible to tourists and therefore rarely crowded.

The newer section of Port Grimaud has the advantage of both the beach and limited car-parking outside your villa, provided that you are given a pass with your key (check in advance with your tour company, if renting from the UK); however, it is remote from the shops, and you need a small motor-boat, which can be hired locally, to get about. The older part of Grimaud has houses of poorer quality, and you have to park outside the main entrance to the marina, controlled by security guards. But the shops and restaurants are within easy walking distance.

A small ferry links Port Grimaud to **St-Tropez**, whose name conjures up a little frisson of excitement that may be repeated when the local restaurant or bar on the fashionable harbour-front brings you your bill. St-Tropez has a limited season, May to October. As the resort faces north, the celebrated mistral wind makes it miserable in the winter months. Most self-catering accommodation consists of elegant villas, located outside the town. Visitors to the resort in summer will find huge traffic jams in both directions on the outskirts and parking a nightmare.

Beyond the Riviera proper, by the less fashionable Corniche des Maures, there are modern villas to rent close to **Cavalaire-sur-Mer**, whose sheltered sandy beach, fringed by huge palm trees, is among the best in the South of France. The better-known **Le Lavandou,** to the east, a mixture of high-rise apartments and terraced villas, is an increasingly popular self-catering centre. Its long, sandy beach is protected by pines, but becomes insufferably crowded in midsummer. Just off the coast, the nudist colony of the **Island of Levant** has many villas to rent in the village of Héliopolis. Be prepared for the local agent to

meet you with the key wearing little more than a
diminutive G-string.

Away from the grand villas and purpose-built
apartments of the Riviera, self-catering accommodation in
the South of France is likely to be based on the traditional
Provençal *mas*, a unique style of stone dwelling
constructed with a minimum of mortar. Although some
such buildings, originally farms, stand in splendid isolation
in deserted countryside, many more are clustered together
to form a defence against enemies of long ago, such as the
Saracens or the Barbary pirates. Wherever possible, the
inhabitants added the natural protection of a hillside, with
buildings literally perched on its slopes – the 'perched'
villages that can be found throughout the south. More
recently, they have been made weatherproof through the
addition of rough plaster in traditional colours of mauve,
orange or pink, with roofs covered with curved, light red
tiles.

If the houses have much in common, the landscape is a
series of sharp contrasts. Perhaps the most beautiful lies
east of the great Roman city of Orange towards the
Dentelles de Montmirail, the exotic 'lace points' that
make up the foothills of the Ventoux range. Forced out of
the earth by some prehistoric convulsion, their peaks have
been honed sharp by the elements. Among the more
interesting places with self-catering accommodation are
Séguret, an artist's retreat built against a rock face,
Carpentras, a hectic agricultural centre with a prodigious
general market, and **Vaison-la-Romaine,** a modern
Provençal town that was previously a sophisticated Roman
city and a medieval stronghold. In Roman times it had a
transient summer population, with houses built
specifically to let: how little changes.

Vaison has fascinating Roman remains, one of many
towns with enduring evidence of the might of the Roman
Empire, spilling over from modern Provence into
Languedoc. In **Orange** itself, the splendid commemorative
arch stood across the road that led to Rome; the Roman
theatre is the only one in Europe to have its mighty façade
intact. The great aqueduct of the Pont-du-Gard, west of

Avignon, demonstrates the genius of Roman engineering.
It was built to carry water 40 miles to **Nîmes,** whose
amphitheatre and temple are the best preserved in the
Roman world. **Arles** has an equally impressive and
slightly larger Roman arena. Vaison-la-Romaine, Orange,
Nîmes and Arles each offers villas nearby and comfortable
self-catering apartments in the town itself. The advantage
of being able to wander among the ruins before the first
tourist bus appears over the horizon may be outweighed in
summer by the sheer volume of visitors, who ensure that
prices are high. Car-parking, too, is difficult at Vaison and
Nîmes, and a positive nightmare in the little streets of
Arles. The police treat foreign cars with a studied
ruthlessness, summoning the towaway truck at the
slightest provocation.

    Avignon also has fine houses to rent a short drive away
and a few flats in the city itself, some within walking
distance of the Palace of the Popes. Their rental, however,
often reflects their scarcity value rather than the quality of
the accommodation. There is ample (though expensive)
parking actually underneath the papal palace, reached by
way of the gate close to the Pont St-Bénézet, the famous
Pont d'Avignon of the song. Avignon's annual
International Drama Festival, which takes place from mid-
July until early August, gives the city a festive air but puts
self-catering property at a premium at that time.

    East of Avignon, many modest properties are available
close to the Lubéron Mountains, much of it a National
Park preserving its wonderful flora and fauna. At the apex
of the hills between the plateau of the Vaucluse and the
Coulon Valley lies the famous village of **Roussillon,** so
called after the red hue of its houses, some of which can be
rented in summer. To the west is **Gordes,** a spectacular
acropolis hewn out of the rock, which has houses nearby.
Further west, there is self-catering accommodation in and
around **Fontaine-de-Vaucluse,** whose underground
spring and beautiful setting beside the river Sorgue are
delightful out of season and a potential nightmare in high
summer, the target of the best part of a million visitors.

    Further south, stay if you dare in the village of **Lacoste,** from whose ruined fortress the infamous Marquis de Sade once struck terror in the hearts of the local population. Or rent a holiday home in the restored medieval village of **Oppède-le-Vieux,** a magical retreat at the end of a remote road that leads nowhere. South of Avignon, on the route to Arles, there are many villas available near **St-Rémy,** and a few apartments in its arcaded streets. Less easy to find, but infinitely rewarding, would be a property near **Les Baux,** the eagle's lair of medieval robber-barons, where only broken ramparts survive. There are houses to rent in the village below, whose population, now a few hundred, once numbered 6000.

South-west of Arles, the reclaimed marshland leads to the reincarnation of medieval France, the town of **Aigues-Mortes,** whose walls are perfectly preserved. It has several good apartments to rent but little property nearby until you reach **Port-Camargue.** A modern resort started in 1969, Port-Camargue has none of the charisma of Port Grimaud but its bungalow accommodation is popular among the yachting folk that use its moorings throughout the summer. In winter it is practically deserted. The season is much longer at **Le-Grau-du-Roi,** a lively and picturesque resort at the mouth of the canal linking Aigues-Mortes to the sea.

Arles is the gateway to the Camargue, a fertile flat region due south, famous for its white horses and relentless mosquitoes. **Saintes-Maries-de-la-Mer** is the principal resort, with many holiday properties and a bustling atmosphere.

Getting there

By air from Heathrow to Nice (1¾ hours) or Marseilles (2 hours); from Manchester to Nice (2¼ hours). Nice's Côte d'Azur airport is four miles west of the city. Marignane airport is 17 miles north-west of Marseilles.

By road, Calais to Nice via the Paris *périphérique*, almost entirely motorway, is about 765 miles. Le Havre to Nice, via Rouen and the Paris *périphérique*, is about 700 miles.

In summer French Motorail (179 Piccadilly, London W1V 0BA; telephone 071-493 9731) operates overnight five times each week between Boulogne and Avignon; and weekly from

Boulogne or Dieppe to Fréjus. There is also a daily Calais–Nice service throughout the year.

Local transport
There are good rail connections along the coast between Marseilles and the Italian border. Buses are crowded with campers in summer and can be caught in huge traffic jams in July and August, especially near St-Tropez. Hire cars are expensive throughout Provence and the Côte d'Azur and need to be reserved well in advance in summer. Beware extremely large taxi fares from Nice airport to destinations along the coast; agree a price in advance.

Weather

Averages	Jan	Feb	Mar	Apr	May	Jun
Temperature	55	55	59	63	68	75
Sun hours	5	6	6	8	9	10
Rainy days	6	7	7	7	5	4
Sea temp.	55	54	55	57	61	68

Averages	Jul	Aug	Sep	Oct	Nov	Dec
Temperature	81	81	77	70	63	55
Sun hours	12	10	9	6	5	4
Rainy days	2	3	5	8	9	8
Sea temp.	72	73	70	66	61	57

Although Provence and the Côte d'Azur are mild from mid-April to November, sustained sunshine is likely only in July and early August. Thunderstorms are common throughout the autumn. The sea is warm from mid-May to the end of September.

Brittany

In the dark mists of time, the Knights of the Round Table are said to have set out for Brittany from Cornwall on their quest to discover the Holy Grail. Unlike the Grail, the link has never quite been lost. Brittany and its Celtic people still have more in common with Cornwall and Wales than with the rest of France. The French are foreigners here, too.

Brittany, or little Britain, is a region of two distinct halves. The north-east has fallen more under the influence of mass tourism, helped by its proximity to the principal ferry ports and the spur of the French 300 kph train, the TGV *Atlantique*. The jagged coast takes the full impact of the Atlantic storms during the winter. The south-west, with its sheltered coastline, retains its Breton language, customs and art, manifested in vivid church decoration – this is the home of the hideous gargoyle.

Sightseeing is limited: there are no places of outstanding interest in Brittany, and few appealing towns. Even the marooned monastery of Mont-St-Michel is just across the border in Normandy. It's the scenery – both inland and coastal – that people come for.

Brittany has a huge number of self-catering properties on offer, combining a coast and country holiday, as very few are far from the sea. Even in high season, Brittany has none of the overcrowding seen on the Riviera and increasingly in the popular inland touring centres of the Loire and the Dordogne. The weather, notoriously unpredictable, is a contributory factor.

Fishing and farming remain Brittany's principal activities, despite its reputation as a holiday region. With a little perseverance, a motorist can find a quiet beach among the multiple nooks and crannies that make up the 2000 miles of Brittany's coastline. But the peace can be broken during the summer, when even the dullest inland village can suddenly spring to life in the season of the pardons, a solemn religious procession ending in much less sacred celebrations.

Every town has a crêperie – crêpes are a speciality of

the region – serving a variety of sweet and savoury pancakes made with buckwheat and Breton butter. The butter, unsalted, is also used to make biscuits, cakes and butter sauces, which accompany many local fish dishes, of which shellfish are often the most spectacular. Brittany has no wine of its own: instead the locals drink cider, altogether a more formidable alcoholic challenge than many of its British counterparts. It looks cloudy, and it can quickly cloud the mind of the unwary.

St-Malo, once the home of pirates that preyed on Channel shipping, is now the main ferry gateway to the region. It has some apartments available within its medieval ramparts, not far from the sandy beach, and agreeable rural properties very close to the town. Some families arrive at their *gîte* just a quarter of an hour after leaving the ferry terminal.

There are further pleasant beaches along the east coast leading to the oyster-harvesting centre but otherwise dull town of **Cancale.** Another cluster of *gîtes* is centred on **Dol-de-Bretagne,** once a seaside bishopric, now inland, insignificant, but charming for all that. Just to the south lies one of Brittany's few imposing châteaux, the fortress of Combourg. The coast road continues east to Normandy and Mont-St-Michel.

The broad estuary of the Rance runs from St-Malo to **Dinan,** whose medieval walls rise high above the valley. It is easy to lose your way in the cobbled maze of the old town, a rewarding visit; self-catering accommodation here is hard to come by. A dam across the Rance connects St-Malo to the fashionable resort of **Dinard,** a favoured destination of the Victorians. It has some grand villas and modest apartments for rent with outstanding sea views; there is little nightlife. For watersport enthusiasts Dinard has a great deal to offer, and its sandy beaches are ideal for children.

The coast road continues west to **St-Lunaire,** which has another fine beach, then **St-Briac,** equally good for bathing; both have many *gîtes* nearby. For more imposing villas, some with splendid gardens, continue to **Lancieux,** whose golf course is a challenge for the best professionals.

BRITTANY

Cancale
Dol-de-Bretagne
St-Malo
St-Lunaire
Dinard
Dinan
St-Jacut-de-la-Mer
St-Briac
Lancieux
St-Cast-le-Guildo
Jugon-les-Lacs
Pléneuf-Val-André
Erquy
Lamballe
Rance
176
St-Brieuc
BRÉHAT
St-Quay-Portrieux
Paimpol
Morlaix
Port-Blanc
Perros-Guirec
Ploumanach
Trégastel-Plage
Ile-Grande
Trebeurden
Locquirec
Huelgoat
786
12
Carantec
Roscoff
St-Pol-de-Léon
Plougastel
Brignogan-Plage
L'Aber-Wrac'h
788
170
788
Brest
Camaret
Morgat
12

0   30km
0   20miles

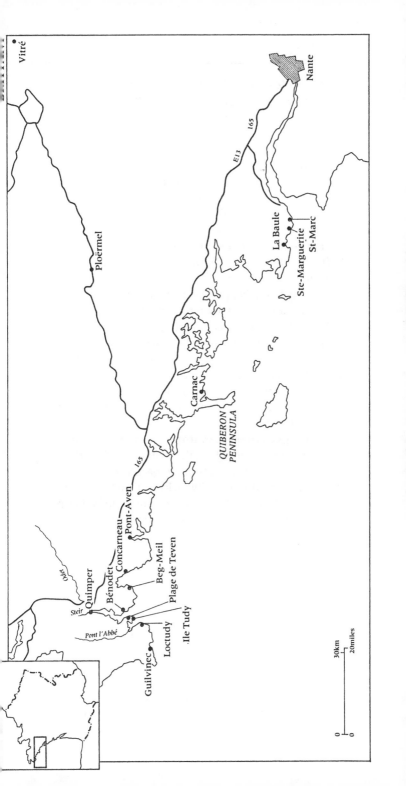

St-Jacut-de-la-Mer has more spartan accommodation on a rather windy promontory; while **St-Cast-le-Guildo** is a favourite for families, with some friendly restaurants clustered around the harbour that shelters both the dwindling fishing fleet and an increasing number of up-market yachts.

Continuing west, a number of modest villas are available at **Erquy,** whose fine seafood restaurants on the sheltered quayside of the old harbour take advantage of the local catch of scallops. Its beaches are pristine sandcastle territory – flat, clammy sand. A short drive south-west, **Pléneuf-Val-André** has one of the best beaches in Brittany.

Many self-catering properties lie within easy reach of **St-Brieuc,** a nondescript town redeemed only by its shopping facilities. To the south-east, more *gîtes* lie close to **Lamballe,** just inland, a small town standing beside a freshwater lake, offering opportunities for sailing and swimming. The coast runs north-west from St-Brieuc to **St-Quay-Portrieux,** an energetic, at times even frenetic resort with some fashionable villas and an active nightlife centred on the casino.

The old fishing port of **Paimpol** has a few Breton cottages to rent overlooking the island of Bréhat, the starting-point of the Pink Granite coast, so called because of the submerged and deadly rocks that emerge, pink-coloured, at low tide. Between here and its finishing-point at **Trebeurden** is a whole series of family resorts, extremely popular with the French, all with self-catering accommodation. **Port-Blanc,** tucked into a sheltered bay, is the prettiest; **Perros-Guirec** is the liveliest; the fishing village of **Ploumanach** the most unspoilt; and **Trégastel-Plage** the best for bathing: it has several small beaches. Just back from the coast, the tranquil village of **Ile Grande** has several nearby *gîtes*. **Locquirec,** west again and well off the beaten track, has an increasingly fashionable marina, which is pushing up the prices.

There are better villas available near **Carantec,** an established resort on a promontory that hedges the east bank of the river Morlaix; Carantec is very exposed in bad weather. The ancient cathedral town of **St-Pol-de-Léon,** deserted by the sea across the centuries, provides a valuable shopping centre for the self-catering holiday-maker. To the north-west, **Roscoff** is the most westerly of the Channel gateway ports from the UK, and much underrated. Its old town has a splendid ambience, and though the port beach is grubby there are several fine beaches nearby. Self-catering accommodation tends to be out of town, to the west. **Brignogan-Plage** has some seaside apartments overlooking its broad sandy bay.

L'Aber-Wrac'h** has a few houses to rent, rather too close to a summer disco, but convenient for the beach. Visitors to this part of Brittany should remember that in winter the full might of the Atlantic crashes against these shores unchecked, when Finistère takes on an ominous ring in the catalogue of gale warnings.

The coast immediately south of the huge port of Brest is best avoided. **Plougastel** has an ugly urban sprawl, **Camaret** gives the (entirely misleading) impression of having seen better days, and **Morgat** is a drab resort despite its long sandy beach.

Further south, **Guilvinec** is a genuine fishing village with few concessions to the tourist; Breton dress is worn and the local dialect spoken out of habit, not artifice. Most of the houses for rent here are not far from the sandy beach, which is sometimes dangerous for inexperienced swimmers because of unsuspected currents. As the coastline tucks itself away from the Atlantic and begins to face south, you arrive at **Ile Tudy,** a little town at the mouth of the river Pont l'Abbé; it has a network of old streets and a thriving atmosphere. Most self-catering accommodation is close to the nearby **Plage de Teven,** whose gentle slope makes it ideal for children, though it is frequently windswept. **Loctudy,** on the other bank, is an unappealing sprawl, and not recommended. **Bénodet,** up the river Odet, is the best resort in this area, offering many activities, including some interesting river-trips, and with an active nightlife. However, some of the best villas have been spoilt by major redevelopment, much of it self-catering, practical rather than aesthetically pleasing.

Quimper, at the confluence of the Odet and the Steir, is a highly popular self-catering centre, though few of the houses on offer are in the charming old town, with its narrow cobbled streets.

The coast now swings south-east to the resort of **Beg-Meil,** bafflingly popular in view of the number of rocks interrupting its duned beach. **Concarneau,** a serious fishing port, has problems with pollution, and much of it should be avoided. But the atmosphere in its small and ancient walled 'cité' is superb, especially at night, when the day-trippers have departed, so it's well worth trying to secure one of the rare self-catering apartments or tiny houses on offer there.

Pont-Aven, once frequently visited by the great artist Paul Gaugin, suffers even more from transitory tourists, but does have a number of attractive houses to rent tucked away in the hills behind. **Carnac,** the centre of the first and mysterious Breton civilisation, has a faded Victorian air; those looking for an activity holiday by day and by night should opt for the adjacent **Carnac-Plage.** It has chic villas with neat gardens, a bustling marina with unfulfilled aspirations to become another Antibes, and some promising, if pricey, restaurants.

Carnac is far superior to the nondescript resorts of the **Quiberon Peninsula,** which have no true sense of identity, and an enforced gaiety that can become tedious during a prolonged stay. However, the facilities are excellent, especially for those who want fishing, riding, sailing or water-skiing. Most self-catering property here is modern and well built. Further south-east, the quiet and unpretentious resorts of **Ste-Marguerite** and **St-Marc** have houses, bungalows and apartments close to sandy beaches, though St-Marc does have a number of inconvenient rocks.

All self-catering in Brittany pales into insignificance when compared to the availability at **La Baule,** the southernmost and sunniest resort whose grand crescent of sand, viewed from the air, resembles in summer a teeming anthill. The best of the self-catering accommodation is in Baule-les-Pins, elegant villas with manicured gardens, mainly French second homes or snapped up for holiday lets from advertisements in Parisian newspapers. However, just a little further down-market, and a little further from the sea, are thousands more villas, some of which can be booked through UK companies. Add the blocks of gleaming white apartments overlooking the resort, and you have nearly 12,500 self-catering units to choose from. La Baule is expensive, reflecting its growing popularity among the more affluent French youth. It caters for people with a thirst to be active on land, sea and in the air (an aero club offers a course for beginners; but check your insurance). It is also extremely noisy at night anywhere close to the sea. This is not the place to be for a quiet, inexpensive family holiday.

Inland Brittany has its own opportunities for aquatic activities, in surroundings much less crowded than on the coast in summer. In the north-west, the village of **Huelgoat** stands on a picturesque lake, complete with waterfall. In the north-west, **Jugon-les-Lacs** is another delightful lakeside town, with large old houses to rent by the water's edge. **Vitré,** in the east, is close to another lake, with a quiet and pleasant beach, ideal for swimming. **Ploërmel,** in the south-east, has a sailing school on its lake and a series of excellent restaurants with the cuisine to match the view.

Getting there

The most convenient route to Brittany is usually by the Channel crossing from Portsmouth to St-Malo, just 43 miles north of the provincial capital, Rennes. It is a long (nine hours) and boring journey, and people may prefer the shorter (four hours) crossing to Cherbourg, which adds a further 85 miles to the same destination. Travellers to Quimper and the southern Brittany coast may find that the Plymouth to Roscoff (six hours) route more convenient; Quimper is about 65 miles from Roscoff. The same destination is just under 130 miles from St-Malo and 250 miles from Cherbourg.

Local transport

Some of the best of Brittany can be seen by boat. From Dinard it takes two hours and a half to reach the island of Cézembre, whose magnificently sandy beach is ample compensation for the choppiest sea. Depending on the tide, it takes roughly as long from Dinard to reach Dinan by way of the river Rance, whose boarded banks provide a fascinating kaleidoscope of disused boatyards and isolated hamlets.

Buses go practically everywhere in Brittany, but rarely during the middle of the day; expect them to be overflowing in summer. They offer useful connections with trains – for example, Carhaix to Guingamp, from where you can be in Paris in little over three hours on the TGV.

Weather

Averages	Jan	Feb	Mar	Apr	May	Jun
Temperature	44	44	49	53	62	65
Sun hours	3	3	5	7	9	8
Rainy days	11	9	10	11	9	10
Sea temp.	39	39	44	48	53	58

Averages	Jul	Aug	Sep	Oct	Nov	Dec
Temperature	69	69	65	58	49	46
Sun hours	8	8	7	5	3	2
Rainy days	10	10	9	11	11	12
Sea temp.	64	64	62	53	44	41

Brittany's south coast is slightly warmer than the north, but the climate resembles Cornwall's: relatively mild, changeable, frequently wet with chilly seas.

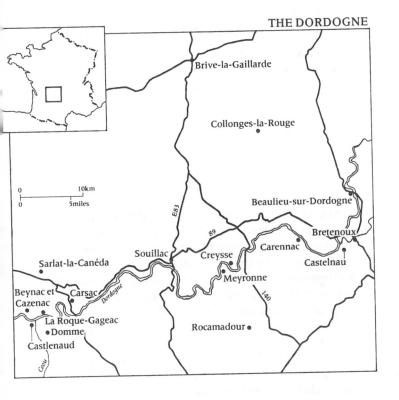

The Dordogne

The Dordogne has many affluent and amiable builders, who have profited handsomely from the British desire for retirement or second homes. The chances are, if you book a self-catering holiday in this region, that the property has been renovated and that the owners will be British. Expect therefore copious instructions on how to relight the boiler or what to do if the washing machine goes on the blink. Do not be surprised if your unpretentious *gîte* has some of the comforts of home, such as a kettle and a teapot. But woe betide you if you forget to water the garden.

There are literally thousands of properties available to rent in the Dordogne, ranging from humble cottages to grand manor houses. No major attraction in the region is

43

far from a cluster of *gîtes* or up-market villas. Even so, the demand is so great at the height of summer that the rental prices continue to rise year after year.

Some rental companies are tempted to stretch the definition of the Dordogne to its outer limits, to take in the entire region of France between the Loire Valley and the river Garonne, deep in the south-west. The Dordogne is both a *département* and a river, but it is the river valley that provides the fabulous scenery and where most visitors, given a choice, prefer to stay.

Begin at **Brive-la-Gaillarde,** a jolly if unremarkable town, but for many the northern gateway to the Dordogne. Just to the south-east is a village that gives a true flavour of the region's infinite capacity to surprise, **Collonges-la-Rouge.** So called because every house was constructed in deep-red stone, the village has been painstakingly restored and preserved. Collonges is sufficiently distanced from the main routes to avoid the pitfalls of mass tourism, and in the evening, when the visitors have departed, it is like a medieval time-capsule. You can, with difficulty, rent a house in the village, but demand always far exceeds the supply.

Continue on back-roads south-east and join the river at **Beaulieu-sur-Dordogne,** an agreeable market town and *gîte* centre with many facilities for sailing and swimming – but no beach. **Bretenoux** to the south offers nearby villas, not far from the ruined fortress of **Castelnau**, a reminder of the time when this was a battleground of the English and the French in the Hundred Years War. After the Dordogne river swings north-west, the picturesque and peaceful village of **Carennac** has ancient houses to rent close to the old priory. As the valley deepens and narrows, the river runs faster beneath crumbling towers south-west to **Creysse,** an exquisite spot at the foot of a rocky spur; accommodation here is hard to find. However, there are houses around **Meyronne,** a hamlet absorbed into the cliff face above an ancient bridge. South-east, the remarkable village of **Rocamadour,** perched precariously like some elderly eagle above a river bed that dried up centuries ago, is an irresistible magnet for tourists. A little self-catering accommodation is available, but most long-term visitors would soon weary of the interminable coach-parties, awful souvenirs and excessive restaurant prices.

The Dordogne continues its violent course north-west where, just removed from the river, the town of **Souillac** is a jolt to the senses, packed with frenetic through traffic. It is an outstanding centre for shopping, with plenty of central car-parks. Now south-west again, the Dordogne grows calmer, almost meandering between the rock basins, past the rural village of **Carsac,** which has *gîtes* nearby. North of the river, **Sarlat-la-Canéda** has a superbly restored medieval quarter with some self-catering accommodation, very atmospheric after dark. This is a busy market town, packed with shoppers, and it is not always easy to park here.

The river quickly turns to a violent rush of water, past golden rocks on which old castles perch like props for a Disney film. High above the bathing places of the Dordogne, the stunning village of **Domme** was once an impenetrable fortress, defended by sheer cliffs on one side and complex ramparts on the other. The narrow streets weave between ancient, ochre houses, wonderfully restored; some may be rented in summer. During the day the transient tourist population becomes hard to bear, but in the evening Domme takes on a magical charm of its own.

Downstream, on another bend of the river, the equally beautiful **La Roque-Gageac** merges into a sheer cliff, many of its houses part golden stone and part original rock. In the Céou Valley, close to the castle of **Castlenaud,** more houses are available to rent, standing in beautiful countryside. North-west, the most memorable stretch of the Dordogne ends in spectacular fashion at **Beynac-et-Cazenac,** whose great stronghold towers above the ancient houses by the riverside.

Getting there

Motorail overnight from Boulogne to Brive-la-Gaillarde is by far
the most painless method of travel. Driving all the way via the
short Channel crossing from Dover to Calais, Brive is just under
500 miles, by motorway via Paris and Tours, then to Limoges and
Sarlet-la-Canéda. The more convenient but longer Channel
crossing is Portsmouth–Le Havre, leaving a journey of just under
400 miles, via Loches and Limoges, but the roads are slower.

Local transport

The major places of interest reach saturation point in July and
August, when parking can be almost impossible. Local buses offer
an attractive alternative, although buses still on the road after
dark are extremely rare. Brive and Cahors are the centres of the
best network of services.

Weather

Averages	Jan	Feb	Mar	Apr	May	Jun
Temperature	50	54	61	64	70	77
Sun hours	4	5	5	7	8	9
Rainy days	13	10	11	8	10	9

Averages	Jul	Aug	Sep	Oct	Nov	Dec
Temperature	79	81	75	66	57	50
Sun hours	10	10	8	5	4	3
Rainy days	8	9	10	10	11	13

The Dordogne has a great deal of sunshine, and long, hot
summers, but it is by no means dry. September, full of crisp
mornings and red sunsets, is perhaps the best month. The winters
are mild but wet.

The Loire

The Loire is a lazy river, too lazy even to meander: its gentle course through a very wide and very flat valley, drained of water in summer, leaves ugly sandbanks in its wake with almost an apologetic air. Except in towns, there are practically no riverside walks: one bank runs into muddy fields, the other has been turned into a steep and inaccessible flood barrier. The truly stimulating scenery of what is popularly known as the Loire Valley in fact lies much closer to its tributaries, the Cher, the Indre and the Vienne, which run through hillsides and woods largely unchanged since the royal landowners of France and England disputed the territory. It is here, when the English were finally thrown out of France, that the great age of the Loire and her châteaux began.

One way or another, self-catering in the Loire Valley is dominated by châteaux. Either they are what the visitor has come to see, or they have some other role to play. Some *gîtes* once were occupied by servants of the local lord, and sit under the shadow of the château. Other houses to rent come into the category of a *manoir* or country house, grand enough to be called a château anywhere except in châteaux country. Finally, there are opportunities to rent a genuine château itself.

Self-catering in a château has an air of fantasy about it: but there is no reason to be overawed. A French château does not have the scarcity value of a British castle: despite the French Revolution, some 6000 are still inhabited, and only 600 of these are formally open to the public. Many of the remainder are available to rent, some through travel companies, but more often through advertisements in French newspapers or magazines.

Some châteaux are terribly run down and are not really suitable for a fortnight's holiday. Others have been partly renovated and are let as a series of apartments, with the remaining rooms left empty. By sharing with friends, it is possible to achieve remarkable economies of scale, as châteaux with 20 bedrooms are by no means uncommon.

THE LOIRE

Orléans

LOIR-ET-CHER

Chambord
Cour-Cheverny
Cheverny
Valençay

Loire

Blois

Chaumont
Montrichard

152

Amboise
Chenonceaux

Cher

St-Aignan
Montrésor

Indrois

76

Vouvray

Loches

A10

Montbazon

Indre

Tours

Villandry

Azay-le-Rideau

Langeais

Rigny-Ussé

Chinon

Vienne

FOREST OF
FONTEVRAUD

Saumur

Montsoreau

Richelieu

15miles

20km

0

0

However, even the largest houses rarely have more than one kitchen, and some châteaux have no modern kitchen at all. The plumbing may be positively medieval. To be sure of what you are getting, either book through a holiday company or make a personal visit in advance.

Study a map: because the Loire region is far from the sea, and most people have only a vague idea of its size and location, some travel companies include properties to rent which are an extremely long way from the Loire itself. Although there are exceptions, the principal châteaux lie in or near the Loire basin between Blois, south-west of Orleáns, and Saumur, east of Tours. If visiting châteaux is an important feature of your holiday, find somewhere to rent in this area; but expect to pay a premium for doing so.

Begin at **Blois,** the principal city of the *département* of Loir-et-Cher, dominated by its huge royal château. There are stylish apartments to rent not far from the old quarter by the Loire, and many houses in the hills nearby. South-east, the village of **Cour-Cheverney** is an exceptionally agreeable place to stay at, with rather fewer tourists than the adjacent **Cheverney,** whose château is famous for its furnishings and its queues. Upstream to the north-east, the prodigious château of **Chambord** is also close to many *gîtes*. Although visitors are free to wander around at their leisure, Chambord could do with some of the furniture at Cheverney, as most of its 440 rooms contain nothing but dust. Downstream, houses to rent are rare near **Chaumont,** a beautiful and much undervalued château.

Amboise also has a fine château, with superb views over the Loire, and is also an attractive country town in its own right. There are fine properties for rent nearby, and the odd apartment in town: but beware traffic noise. On the north bank, **Vouvray,** famed for its sparkling wine, is an otherwise nondescript village. The Loire leads into **Tours,** the geographical centre of the region, which has all the advantages and disadvantages of a large town: excellent shopping, but a far from relaxing atmosphere. *Gîtes* are available nearby, and some apartments in town: the latter are not recommended in summer, when Tours suffers from a surfeit of visitors. Coach-tour holidays, in particular, use Tours as a staging-post, arriving late at night and leaving, with much revving of engines, at the crack of dawn.

Tours lies close to the confluence of the Loire and its tributary the Cher, on which, to the south-east, sits the marvellous château at **Chenonceaux,** an architectural masterpiece. The château caters admirably for visitors, with no guided tours, plenty of information in English and, in July and August, even a children's nursery. Unfortunately, the same cannot be said for its overpriced adjoining village, which has practically no self-catering accommodation and problems with coach-parties leaving their hotels at first light on the next stage of their tour.

To the east, the thriving market town of **Montrichard** is a much more promising base from which to visit the château. It has pleasant river walks, and its own beach, not far from the bridge. Some of its old houses can be rented. Nearby, **St-Aignan,** another attractive riverside town, has property available on the wooded slopes beneath its château. Away from the Cher, striking south, the classic château of **Valençay** also marks a cluster of self-catering accommodation, some in the village itself. West of Valençay the château of **Montrésor** dominates another riverside village, this time on the Indrois, a tributary of the Indre. It has the advantage of comparatively few visitors and is a good *gîte* centre. The Indre itself is a beautiful river, wandering through thickly wooded and chalk escarpments. Due west of Montrésor, it passes beneath **Loches,** an interesting two-tiered town, modern beside the river, medieval on the rocky hill above. Most accommodation is in the modern part, which is a pity as the old quarter has most of the really elegant property and an atmosphere of dignified tranquillity. North-west, where the Indre veers away from Tours, more self-catering properties are concentrated in the area close to the ruined keep of **Montbazon,** a quiet town on both banks of the river.

At **Azay-le-Rideau,** not far short of the junction of the Indre and the Loire, the popularity of its beautiful château ruins the ambience of the village, where accommodation is overpriced and restaurants particularly expensive. At the point where the Loire and the Cher divide, just south of Tours, the château of **Villandry,** with its superb restored Renaissance garden, stands close to more self-catering properties. The D7 runs south of the Loire through a number of peaceful and attractive villages, which is more than can be said for the N152 on the north bank, an extremely busy road full of commercial vehicles. Much of this traffic passes through **Langeais,** a large, noisy and disagreeable town despite its formidable château: well worth avoiding.

Further south-west, and on the south bank, the Loire passes the Disney-like château of Usse in the tranquil village of **Rigny-Ussé,** close to several rural *gîtes.* The countryside here is a dense forest of oak, similar to what much of England must have been like in the Middle Ages, stretching almost to the outskirts of **Chinon.** An agreeable town bisected by another Loire tributary, the Vienne, Chinon has a good range of apartments and houses, including some among the streets of the picturesque old quarter beneath the ruined château. It is, however, a popular place for summer visitors and by no means cheap. A steam railway runs in summer to **Richelieu,** once the satellite town of the now-vanished château belonging to the great cardinal. Some elegant houses in its geometrical streets are available to rent.

Almost exactly where the Vienne meets the Loire, the château of **Montsoreau** marks another fertile area for *gîtes* on the edge of the Forest of Fontevraud. The Loire swings north-west to **Saumur,** famous for its sparkling wine but not for its beauty. The town, spreading across both banks of the river, has a number of undistinguished apartments and is of much better value as a convenient shopping centre.

Getting there
By the shortest Channel crossing, Dover to Calais, the Loire can be reached almost entirely by motorway, via Paris to Tours, some 330 miles. By the longer Portsmouth to Le Havre Channel crossing, it is only about 200 miles via Alençon to Tours, but the roads are much slower.

Local transport

For anyone without a car, Tours offers the best network of bus and coach services, particularly excursions to a variety of châteaux. During summer weekends, and on public holidays, a delightful steam train runs twice a day between Chinon and Richelieu, complete with ancient rolling stock.

Weather

Averages	Jan	Feb	Mar	Apr	May	Jun
Temperature	45	46	55	61	66	73
Sun hours	3	4	4	6	7	8
Rainy days	13	10	11	9	9	8

Averages	Jul	Aug	Sep	Oct	Nov	Dec
Temperature	77	75	70	61	52	45
Sun hours	9	9	8	4	3	2
Rainy days	8	8	7	10	11	13

The Loire Valley has mild but very damp winters. The summers are hot, with September potentially the best month, when rain is comparatively rare.

Paris

Apartments in Paris are available from holiday companies or from newspaper advertisements. Some are within sight of the Eiffel Tower, or may be in less salubrious areas, such as Pigalle and around the Gare du Nord. They vary sharply in quality and location, and brochure descriptions in both respects can be particularly misleading. In every case, before confirming a booking it is advisable to check the number of rooms and facilities on offer and the precise address, so you can establish its position on a Paris street map (available from most major bookshops).

If the location is a main street, check whether the bedrooms are at the front, as traffic noise can ruin your stay, especially during the summer when you may wish to keep the windows open.

If the apartment is above the first floor, check whether there is a lift in good working order.

If the apartment has a concierge, check whether temporary residents have a key to the front door for easy access after he or she has gone to bed.

Check whether you are expected to pay for the electricity and gas, and, if so, whether they work on a meter system with coins.

If a telephone is important to you, check whether it has been programmed to take incoming calls only. Flats with telephones invariably involve the occupant paying a substantial deposit, which is refunded only after telephone bills have been presented.

Check the kitchen appliances. Most Paris flats have a washing machine but few have a dishwasher and practically none has a tumble-drier.

Check the arrangements for disposing of rubbish. Some Paris apartments have a waste disposal chute connected directly to rubbish containers.

If you intend arriving in Paris by car, check whether you are entitled to use an enclosed courtyard or lock-up garage while staying in the apartment, and the procedure for collecting the key.

Finding your way into Paris and somewhere to park is less of a problem than may be apparent at first. Many people suppose that the ring road, the *boulevard périphérique*, is routed far from the most popular parts of Paris, when in fact it runs within four blocks of the Arc de Triomphe. Take the A1 Autoroute almost to the Porte de la Chapelle, then take a right filter on to the *périphérique* going west and leave it at the Porte Maillot exit, filtering right and passing under the *périphérique*. Porte Maillot is a huge, circular boulevard, with traffic running anticlockwise. It has two car-parks, one on the south side, to which you come initially, and one on the north side, immediately in front of the Palais des Congrès. If these should be full, two further car-parks are close by, one to the north, just past the Palais des Congrès, on the right-hand side, and one to the south, down the avenue de Malakoff, across the avenue Foch, at the start of a one-way street, the rue de la Pompe. You would have to be extremely unfortunate not to find a space in one of these four car-parks, and having disposed of your vehicle, the Arc de Triomphe is only two stops from Porte Maillot on the Paris underground, the Métro.

For the more adventurous, parking near your apartment in the centre of Paris is still possible, but requires an element of luck. Ask whether your apartment is situated in the inner 'grey' zone, which is practically all meters, expensive and inconvenient, or in the 'blue' zone, which has some free parking but otherwise limits parking to one hour, or two between midday and 2 p.m. There are no restrictions between 7 p.m. and 9 a.m.

Getting there

Flights to Paris operate from all London (1 hour) and major provincial airports (1½–2 hours), in almost every case to Charles de Gaulle airport, 19 miles north-east of the city centre. A free transfer bus connects with Roissy station, from where trains run to the Gare du Nord, and airport buses go direct to the Gare de l'Est and the place de la Nation.

The A26 motorway runs just outside Calais to join the A1 motorway to Paris.

Trains from the Channel ports arrive in Paris at the Gare du Nord.

Local transport

The Métro remains the cheapest and fastest way to get around Paris, although you will see more from a bus. The same tickets are valid for both, and sold at a discount if you buy a book of ten – a *carnet*. Tourist tickets are also available; these offer first-class travel on the Métro, which is much more comfortable during the morning and evening rush-hour.

Weather

Averages	Jan	Feb	Mar	Apr	May	Jun
Temperature	43	47	54	61	68	73
Sun hours	2	3	5	7	8	8
Rainy days	10	9	7	6	8	9

Averages	Jul	Aug	Sep	Oct	Nov	Dec
Temperature	77	75	70	61	50	45
Sun hours	8	7	6	4	2	1
Rainy days	8	9	8	8	8	9

A dry month in Paris is a rarity. The summers are hot, sometimes unpleasantly so, and the winters cold. April in Paris is the most likely time to find mild, sunny weather.

Greece

The Greek islanders have a nonchalent attitude to life epitomised by their favourite and, it must be said, contagious occupation: watching the rest of the world go by. Nothing is ever done today that can be safely put off until tomorrow. However, such is the enthusiasm with which they receive visitors that the lack of planning and maintenance somehow never seems to matter.

It should be said bluntly that there is no such thing as a truly luxurious villa in Greece regularly available for rent. If a brilliantly appointed house is what you want, with immaculate décor and full-size swimming-pool, look elsewhere. Greek villas and apartments are generally shabby, uncomfortably furnished, with mediocre equipment and facilities. If there is a swimming-pool, rare in itself, it may be cracked or even empty. Only houses at the very top of the range come up to what would be regarded as an average standard in other Mediterranean countries such as France and Italy.

The standard of utensils provided will in most cases be poor, with a predominance of cheap glass and plastic. Local agents are extremely reluctant to go through inventories, and seem to take the view that it is less hassle if they simply replace broken items rather then bother with the paperwork.

If you can, find out before you book when the villa on offer was built. If it was completed within the last ten years, the chances are it will have bland architecture, designed to maximise the number of bedrooms, and be totally lacking in character. Older villas are more often closer to the sea, with superior wooden furniture, real marble floors and a patio shaded by mature trees or vines.

Apartments are likely to possess more modern equipment, but almost invariably have excessively thin walls. Bathrooms rarely possess baths, but have showers instead, and hot water sometimes comes from solar heating, itself dependent on sunny weather. Electrical heating systems are subject to interruptions in the power supply, or may be regulated by timer devices incorporated by the owner with economy in mind. Hot water tanks fuelled by portable gas bottles often operate only when switched on and cannot be pre-programmed. Self-catering accommodation that guarantees a hot early-morning shower is extremely rare.

However, if you are looking for really cheap accommodation, Greece is the place to visit. Many villages, especially on the islands, have rooms to rent, sometimes called taverna rooms, literally located over the local restaurant. You may well have access to a simple ring or two for cooking, and be allowed to store your own perishable food in the fridge. The furnishings will be extremely basic, often without a wardrobe, and you will have to share the bathroom with strangers. But if you intend to eat out and spend your time sightseeing or on the beach, none of these disadvantages may really matter.

What to take with you

If, in common with the great majority of holiday-makers, you intend to travel to Greece by air, keep your luggage light: for much of the year the climate is too hot for carrying heavy bags, and on the larger islands most of the comforts of home are readily available. Instant coffee (*Neskafe*) and tea no longer seem significantly more expensive, although if you have a favourite blend you may prefer to take your own. If you are not prepared to make tea in a saucepan, pack your own teapot, no more commonly available in Greece than in any other foreign holiday destination.

Camera film is more expensive than it is in the UK, and local film processing is to be avoided if you take pride in your prints. Cornflakes and proper marmalade (*marmeladha portokali*) remain scarce outside the most popular holiday areas.

To avoid spending time in dull shops, it is preferable, but not essential, to buy toilet items in the UK, including aspirin, antiseptic cream, plasters, calamine lotion, diarrhoea remedy, insect repellent and sting relief creams, and suntan oil if you like a particular level of protection.

Do not assume that your villa or apartment will possess a tin-opener or corkscrew that actually work; take them with you, together with some plastic egg-cups (unknown in Greece), at least one sharp kitchen knife (but do not carry it in your hand baggage), a pair of pliers for emergency repairs, a small adjustable spanner for connecting cooking-gas bottles, a torch with new batteries, and a set of small screwdrivers with a single changeable handle.

Take an adaptor, or some standard Continental two-pin plugs, for use with a hair-drier or electric razor. Most of Greece has now been equipped with the uniform UK 220-volt AC supply, although a few remote islands are still on the 110-volt DC and therefore unsuitable for UK electrical items.

Carry your hand luggage in a strong cool-bag and take, unfrozen, some plastic ice-packs that can be refrozen in the freezer compartment of your refrigerator. The cool-bag can then be used for beach parties and picnics to keep food and drink cold, which will make everything much more appetising.

If you are staying in simple rooms, there may be nowhere to hang your clothes. Take some plastic bags to keep them in, some lightweight hangers and a length of cord to make your own clothes-line.

Eating in

Supermarkets: the word is used internationally and in Greece can describe anything from a huge mainland hypermarket to an island corner shop. Traditionally, a Greek supermarket will stock essential household goods and a wide range of groceries. In more remote areas it may still be described as *bakaliko*, or grocer's. Supermarkets that also sell fruit and vegetables are sometimes called *pantopolio*.

Greengrocers (in Greek, *manaviko*) sometimes sell household groceries as well, particularly on the islands where vegetables are far from plentiful. Unwary tourists are often palmed off with inferior produce.

Fishmongers *(ichthiopolio)* are often little more than a stall in an open-air market on the quayside. Fresh fish goes off quickly in hot weather, so make your purchase early in the morning. The best and most expensive fish available in Greek waters include red mullet (*barbounia*), sea-bream (*fangri*), sea-bass (*lavraki*) and dentex (*sinagridha*). The fishmonger will gut your fish for a small fee. Frozen fish, much cheaper of course, can be bought in supermarkets and, surprisingly, at butchers.

Butchers (*hasapiko*) sell chicken and vegetables as well as meat and frozen fish. Most meat is kept refrigerated, and you may have to insist on seeing what you are buying before it is wrapped. To ensure you get quality meat, specify that it is for roasting (*yia psito*) however you actually intend to cook it. Lamb (*arnaki*) is usually the best buy and pork (*hirino*) the cheapest, as other meat is largely imported. If you buy chicken (*kotopoulo*), ask the butcher to remove the giblets, as chicken is usually sold whole.

Bakers (*fournos*) sell cakes, biscuits and pastries as well as a variety of loaves, which are freshly baked twice a day. Instead of *croissants* for breakfast, try *tsoureki,* a sweet-tasting breadcake.

Eating out

Greek cuisine has the reputation, unfairly, for being poor. This reputation arises from the separate but entirely justified fact that the Greeks can, in culinary terms, fleece gullible tourists, who, when it comes to cooking, often get the food that they deserve.

Tourists mistakenly think that the average Greek sits down for lunch at 1 p.m. and for dinner at 7 p.m., whereas the average Greek is sleeping soundly at 1 p.m. and still working at 7 p.m. It follows that only tourists want to eat at these hours and can be fobbed off with indifferent food. If they choose not to come back, well, another group of tourists will be along the following day.

Tourists also fail to appreciate that Greek chefs have their limitations: they have almost no idea how to make the well-known international dishes. Only Athens, its nearby coastline and Thessaloniki (Salonika) possess first-class restaurants run by trained professionals, where the décor, napery and silverware are the trappings of a superb meal served gracefully in elegant surroundings.

If you have lunch, start eating at 2.30 or 3 p.m. Dine out at 9 p.m. or even later at the height of summer, when the temperature will be much more pleasant in any case.

Choose a restaurant that is unpretentious, even primitive. Any restaurant offering other than wooden tables, hard chairs, paper tablecloths and napkins, and wine glasses that would look more at home holding a toothbrush should be regarded with suspicion.

Do not be surprised if no menu is provided. This usually means that you are expected to visit the kitchen to look at the food and make a personal choice.

Do not be surprised if the food is luke-warm. Greek restaurants do most of their cooking in the morning and see nothing amiss with keeping the dishes warm until they are eaten. Grilled meat and fish will always be cooked to order, though.

If there is a menu, you will usually find two prices after each dish. The lower price is the tax-free price, but the higher price will always be charged. By law, this price includes a service charge. The idea of 'courses' is incomprehensible to a Greek waiter, who will bring starters, salads and main courses all together or in a hopelessly wrong order: the solution is to order the food in the sequence in which you will eat it.

Waiters are no more efficient when it comes to making up the bill. They seldom write down an order and often at the end of the meal can be seen peering at the scraps left on your plates to see what you have eaten. The bill, even for those fluent in Greek, is usually illegible. But eating out in Greece is, by British standards, exceptionally cheap.

However rough and ready they may be, Greek restaurants fall into different categories. *Estiatoria* serve sophisticated dishes such as grilled meats and fish, pasta and stews, do more of their trade at lunchtime and usually expect people to eat indoors. *Tavernas* generally consist of little more than an indoor kitchen with tables in the street or garden.

Psarotavernas specialise in fish, of which the prime dishes are the same as the fresh fish already mentioned. Also worth trying are *kalamarakia*, fried baby squid. *Psistaries* specialise in grills, particularly spit-roasted lamb, which in any taverna is a reliable choice, especially as lamb *souvlakia* (shish-kebab).

Before you eat, sample – but with caution – the traditional Greek aperitif *ouzo*, with its strong aniseed flavour. *Ouzo* remains clear until mixed with water, when it turns a milky colour. Greek bars and restaurants usually serve two glasses, one neat *ouzo*, the other water, so that you can decide for yourself how strong you like it.

To wash down the meal, try the traditional Greek white wine *retsina* or its rosé equivalent, *kokineli*. *Retsina*, a golden-yellow colour, acquires its unique taste by the addition of pine resin during fermentation. Many island tavernas draw it straight from barrels fixed at strategic intervals around the walls. Another favoured wine is Demestica, from Patras; the red Demestica has a rather sharp taste, but the white is mild and extremely palatable. Wine produced by the large Greek vineyards maintains a high quality: brand names to look out for include Boutari,

Kambas Blanc, Kourtakis and Mount Hymettus. Local specialities are listed under the individual islands.

After dinner, Greek brandy can send you home happy but result in a horrendous hangover. The best brandy, Metaxa, is produced with three, five and seven stars, the last of which connoisseurs of French brandy claim to be the equivalent of a two-star cognac. But at least it is a genuine local product. Greek beer is simply an international brand of lager brewed – sometimes badly – under licence.

Children

Children are welcome everywhere, especially in restaurants, and no one expects them either to keep quiet or to sit still. If they cannot be persuaded to eat traditional Greek dishes, hamburgers or chicken with chips are practically always available.

Most supermarkets, except in the most remote islands, carry disposable nappies, powdered milk and international brands of baby food.

For babysitters, try the local representative of the villa or apartment renting company, or the owner. If that fails, a small tip to the porter at a large local hotel will often produce a babysitter, often one of the hotel maids. In the islands, ask at the local supermarket.

Incidentally, child-molesters are practically unknown among the indigenous Greek population, so the need to keep an eye on your children should be largely determined by the presence of fellow foreigners.

Transport

If your villa or apartment is offered with the recommendation that you hire a car, what that means is that life there without a car will be quite impractical. Car hire is expensive in Greece, and the cheapest method may be to arrange it through your tour company. If you are travelling independently, and are tempted to rent from a small local firm, always make sure that the quoted price includes local taxes and a collision damage waiver so that you are covered in full against any accident. Greeks drive on the right – most of the time. . .

Buses are cheap and reliable, but most of the services are crammed into a few hours of the day. They start at dawn, often stop running mid-morning, then begin again mid-afternoon.

Taxis are much cheaper than they are in the UK, and drivers are quite relaxed about people sharing, which pushes the cost down still further.

Scooters and bicycles are often in poor condition and extremely vulnerable to accidents, so they are not recommended.

Ferries between local islands often consist of small caiques, which run unpredictably and can be hired on demand.

Long-distance ferries between Piraeus, the port of Athens, and the major islands have a fixed timetable that is often subject to disruption. Check with the local shipping office and keep an eye out to sea: the sailing you want is just as likely to be a day early as late.

Domestic flights operate from Athens airport to many of the major islands. In season they are heavily in demand and overbooked in both directions to compensate for full-fare passengers who fail to turn up. Even with a firm booking, to be sure of a seat it is essential to check in early. Domestic and all Olympic Airways flights use the East terminal of Athens airport; all other flights, including charter flights, use the West terminal. The two terminals are linked by road, and getting from one to the other takes at least 15 minutes by bus or taxi.

Avoiding problems

Although Greece is a member of the EC and extends reciprocal medical treatment for visitors, the bureaucracy involved in reclaiming the cost remains considerable. The best advice is to take out full holiday insurance cover, which also improves the quality of medical care available.

For emergency medical treatment, in most places dial

166 or ring the tourist police (see below). It is important to emphasise to a doctor, who may otherwise be reluctant to make a home visit, that his fee will be paid on the spot and reclaimed later.

Local chemists (*farmakio*), found in all but the very smallest islands, are marked by a green cross on a white background. They can prescribe drugs but should be treated with caution, especially where children are concerned. In Greece strong drugs are administered with far less consideration of the consequences than in Britain.

The tourist police is an English-speaking branch set up in most major holiday areas to assist visitors with problems. In some places they will also help to find accommodation. Dial 171 wherever you are in Greece.

Opening hours
Most shops are open from 8 a.m. to 1 p.m. and from 5 p.m. to 8 p.m. or later in resort areas. Some food shops stay open all day, and are open on Sunday mornings. In the larger resorts some shops take one or more half-days, opening from 8 a.m. to 2 p.m.

Banks are open from 8 or 8.30 a.m. to 1 p.m. or 2 p.m., Monday to Friday. In the main resort areas they also take it in turns to open again from around 5 p.m. to 7 p.m. for currency changing only, and again from 10 a.m. to noon on Saturday mornings. There are long queues at many banks in summer.

Public holidays
1 January (*Agios Vasillis*, Feast of St Basil); **6 January** (*Theophania*, Epiphany); **25 March** (Independence Day); **Good Friday** and **Easter Sunday** (the Orthodox calender, so Easter is about a month after our own); **1 May** (Labour Day); **Whit Sunday** and **Monday** (50 days after Easter); **15 August** (*Panagia*, the Feast of the Assumption of the Virgin Mary); **28 October** (*Ochi Day*, celebrating Prime Minister Metaxas' 'No!' ('*Ochi!*') to Mussolini's request to allow Italian troops right of way through Greece in the Second World War); **25 December** (Christmas Day); **26 December** (*Agios Stephanos*, Feast of St Stephen).

What to bring back
Jewellery
Embroidery
Metalwork
Onyx
Basketwork
Pottery
Porcelain
Glass
Hand-woven cloth
Orange honey
Olive oil
Sandals

Tour operators
For details see page 213

Aer Lingus Holidays
Airlink Holidays
Allegro Holidays
Amathus
Arista Holidays
Beach Villas
Club Cantabrica
Corfu à la Carte
Cosmos
CV Travel
European Villas
Falcon Holidays
Freelance Holidays

Global Air Holidays
Grecian Holidays
Greco-file
Horizon Holidays
Intasun Holidays
Kosmar Villa Holidays
Lancaster Holidays
Leisure Villas
Manos Holidays
Martyn Holidays
Medina Holidays
Meon Travel
Meridian Tours
Olympic Holidays
Pan World Holidays
Pure Crete
Redwing Holidays
RentaVilla
Secker, Catherine
Simply Crete
Skytours
Something Special Travel
Starvillas
Sunseekers
Sunvil Travel
Thomson Holidays
Tjaerborg
The Travel Club
Twelve Islands
VillaSeekers

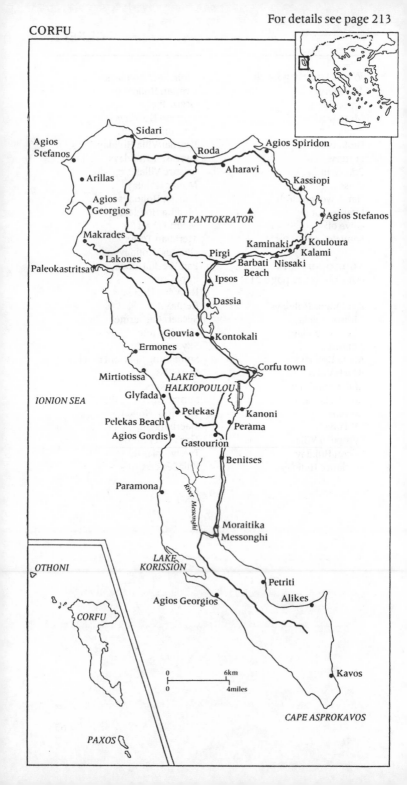

For details see page 213

CORFU

Corfu

The greenest of all the Greek islands, Corfu is in many respects a self-catering paradise. Apart from a few isolated exceptions, the hotels are cheap and rudimentary, and the best accommodation consists of villas and apartments. Even here, visitors should be prepared for manifestations of local life. According to mainland Greeks, the people of Corfu, the Corfiots, have inherited the worst characteristics of their erstwhile conquerors. Thus, they claim maliciously, the Corfiots possess the integrity of Venetians, the humility of the French and the spontaneity of the British. They could have added, much more plausibly, that the Corfiots have transformed delay into an art form. This will only become apparent should you require a remedy or a repair, as the Corfiot plumber will never stop a leak today that can become a bigger and more lucrative leak tomorrow.

Unlike the rest of Greece, Corfu is not a place at which to take pot luck with self-catering accommodation unless you are prepared to be disappointed. Most of the better villas and flats are booked for the full summer season by the major operators, and are rarely available for local lets. From mid-July through August the island is close to saturation point, and not even the local travel agents who ply their trade in the most unlikely of remote fishing villages will be able to find you somewhere to stay.

The capital, **Corfu town**, or Kerkyra, a blend of Italianate houses and French colonnades, has a great many rooms to let and a few apartments, of which the best are in the old town towards the harbour. Corfu town should be regarded as only a base for touring, though, as the nearest beach, in Garitsa Bay, is both artificial and untidy.

Tourists trying for something better who strike south are also in for a disappointment. At the bottom of a peninsula that was once one of the island's beauty-spots stands **Kanoni**, Corfu's contribution to a list of architectural disasters. Its high-rise hotel and apartment blocks have disfigured the landscape. The airport is so close that some of the hotel swimming-pools actually overlook the runway, with the dubious advantage that you could watch your plane land and still have time for a last swim before leaving for home. For several hours in high season on Mondays and Saturdays, the peak periods for flight arrivals and departures, conversation in Kanoni borders on the impossible.

Perama, south across the narrow lip of the inlet known as Lake Halkiopoulou, also suffers acutely from aircraft noise and is best avoided. Its pebble beach, bulldozed out of the cliff's face, is backed by a scrappy row of tavernas (most offering rooms) along the coast road.

This area of Corfu is so overdeveloped that it is difficult to see where one settlement ends and the next begins. The road leads south to **Benitses**, once a charming village whose original streets and inhabitants have been swamped by the package-tour overspill. The scenery is mediocre, the beach largely shingle and horribly cramped in high season. However, for the young holiday-makers who congregate here these things scarcely seem to matter. During the day every conceivable watersport, including scuba-diving, is available, and at night the main road that backs on to the beach comes alive.

This is not the place for a quiet stay, because if the wrecked synchromesh of the local lorries does not keep you awake, then the music certainly will. More than 40 bars stay open for most of the night, some of them self-styled discos with rudimentary sound systems. Spiros, right on the beach, is reckoned the best, but more curious visitors may prefer the action at the Achillion casino near the village of **Gastourion**, two miles out of the centre. The Achillion was built in neo-Gothic style before the turn of the century by Elizabeth, Empress of Austria, who was later assassinated. As the next owner, Kaiser Wilhelm, barely escaped with his life at the end of the First World War, it was never a lucky place, as most modern-day gamblers doubtless discover.

Continuing south, the villages of Moraitika and Messonghi, surrounded by groves of ancient olive trees, are separated by the mouth of the River Messonghi.

Moraitika, split by the main road, has a sprinkling of tavernas (with rooms) and discos, and the advantage of a quite spacious sandy beach, albeit a healthy ten-minute walk. **Messonghi**'s beach is a mixture of sand and shingle and is noticeably wider. Most of the accommodation is back from the road, but still suffers severely from all-night bars and discos.

You can rent rooms at **Petriti**, a tiny fishing village off the beaten track, and around the marshy bay at **Alikes**, which has a sandy beach. But neither has anything for people to do at night, and the countryside is flat and uninteresting. Many of the best self-catering villas on the island can be found further south at **Kavos**, which has fine views of the Greek mainland and a growing number of waterside tavernas along the safe, sandy beach. You can escape from the madding crowd here simply by walking through a series of small coves.

Little caiques run from Kavos to the tiny island of **Paxos**, ten miles south, which boasts six policemen, four taxis, three priests, two battered old buses and one tourist office with literally hundreds of rooms to rent. Just about all the 2000 inhabitants are in the holiday-let business, and in the summer there still are not enough rooms to meet the demand. By using the caique visitors get round the rule that requires travellers from Corfu town by the official ferry to book (and at a premium) two nights' accommodation in advance. Most of the rooms are in the capital, Gaios, which has some agreeable tavernas that come alive after the day-trippers leave for home.

The road to the south of Corfu runs out short of **Cape Asprokavos**, the sandy tip of the island already selected for further villa development but for the moment still unspoilt. Less so is Agios Georgios, which in true Corfiot style is one of two beach resorts on this island bearing exactly the same name. The southernmost **Agios Georgios**, on the south-west coast, is an artificial development of restaurants and discos, rising suddenly out of scrubland on the edge of two exceptional sandy beaches, and serving the growing villa population.

Lake Korission forces the road back inland to Agios

Mattheos, where a rough spur flanked by olive groves leads to the quiet fishing village of **Paramona**. Its jolly taverna rents out rooms, most of the weekend visitors speak Greek, and the village is still largely untouched by the mainstream tourist trade. The same, alas, cannot be said of **Agios Gordis** to the north, a lovely setting swamped by its large cliffside hotel and villa development. The sandy beach touches saturation point in midsummer.

From here the road winds northwards through the black forest of Agios Kontogialos to the hilltop village of **Pelekas**, where the room prices are rising, reflecting the growing demand. The scenery is superb but marred somewhat by the evening arrival of coachloads of tourists on excursions from Corfu town, come to see the spectacular sunset. **Pelekas Beach**, directly below the village, has many uninhibited young visitors who throw clothes and caution to the winds.

Glyfada, slightly to the north-west, is greatly superior to its namesake, the notorious mainland resort on the Athens airport flightpath. Now a favoured self-catering centre, Corfu's Glyfada has all the trappings of package tourism: a tarmac road, a large hotel, several restaurants and a wide variety of watersports, including at the southern end a popular sailing club. Glyfada's principal disadvantage is its proximity to Corfu town, ten miles directly across the island. Day-trippers pack the place in midsummer. For all that, the sandy beach is superb, and the shallow water ideal for children.

Mirtiotissa, a little further north, has a wide beach of golden sand, dramatic surf and wonderful wooded scenery; but it and its tavernas are crowded during the main season. The Hotel Miramare Beach, about a mile from the village, has single-storey self-catering bungalow accommodation available to the independent traveller as well as to the package tourist.

The road winds north-eastwards to **Ermones**, whose undistinguished beach leads directly on to Corfu's main golf course. The hotels at Glyfada tend to hog the greens with guests on inclusive golfing packages, but you can just turn up and play for a modest fee. From **Lakones**, a hilltop village to the north-west, take in the spectacular view of **Paleokastritsa**, a superb combination of bays and beaches, with hotels and villas strung out along the winding approach road to the sea. Paleokastritsa means 'old castle', which still exists, a silent reminder of more turbulent times. Scuba-diving enthusiasts consider that the water here is exceptionally clear. Odysseus is said to have been shipwrecked and washed ashore between the two headlands, where today the fishermen hang out their wooden lobster-pots. Some of their produce is available in the local restaurants, but it is never cheap. In all, Paleokastritsa, only 45 minutes by fast road from Corfu town, consists of four coves, some of sand and others of sand and pebble. The best beaches are immediately below the old castle; they become very busy in midsummer, and the way down is steep.

Another path leads from the nearby village of **Makrades**, which has cheap rooms, to the second **Agios Georgios**. It has one of the best sandy beaches on the island, but the message has reached tourists and developers alike: the tavernas are moving up-market along with their prices, there are signs of substantial self-catering development, and there is a bustling day-tripper business by boat from Paleokastritsa. The tarmac road has also transformed the tiny resorts to the north, **Agios Stefanos** and **Arillas**. Both have adequate sandy beaches; Arillas is slightly more up-market, with a flourishing marina.

From Agios Stefanos (which also has a namesake on the east coast) the road cuts inland to the north-coast resort of **Sidari** (Sidarion), still popular with middle-class Athenians, but singularly dull, with no discernible nightlife. Its solitary street, which offers basic rooms above charming but unsophisticated restaurants, overlooks the beach, a mixture of sand and shingle sloping gently into the sea. A caique runs between Sidari and **Othoni**, a tiny island off the north-west coast, some of whose 400 fishermen rent out rooms during the summer.

The main road turns east among the olive groves, close to the sea, but much of the duned coastal strip has merged with mudbanks thrown up by strong currents. The first safe bathing beach, at **Roda**, has some flats to rent but is dominated by large hotels, and you have to cross the bay to **Aharavi** to find the best self-catering accommodation, a series of smart apartments. **Agios Spiridon** has the most northerly beach in Corfu, but be warned: it is deluged at weekends by Corfiots in their cars, and the tavernas are packed. The rest of the week Spiridon is extremely quiet, although some new self-catering development behind the village could change all that. The sandy beach is tiny but extremely safe, with shallow water for more than a hundred yards, ideal for young children.

Kassiopi, on the north-east coast, has changed from a quiet fishing village to a bustling resort with a flourishing nightlife. It has a particular emphasis on self-catering accommodation, which sometimes suffers from noise from local discos. The best beaches – small coves interspersed with rocks – are remote from the village. The other village called **Agios Stefanos**, with its picture-postcard harbour, has a delicatessen and the latest British newspapers, catering for the occupants of a string of new villas built in the hills above.

The twin bay of **Kouloura** is crammed with fishing boats, some of which now operate adventurous trips to Albania, a mere two miles away. British visitors may care to note that while the Albanian authorities now seem to be turning a blind eye to day-trippers, staying overnight without registering with the police is considered a serious offence, and there is no friendly British consul to visit you in jail. Back in the safety of Corfu, you can eat and drink in the 'white house' made famous by the British author Lawrence Durrell, now converted into the seaside taverna of slumbering **Kalami**. The beaches consist almost entirely of white pebble – hard on the feet. Just as hard is the climb out of **Kaminaki**, a seaside hamlet tucked away at the bottom of a precipitous slope.

The next village, **Nissaki**, lies in a remote cove lapped by an exquisite blue-green sea; but despite its long, narrow, pebble beach the facilities are too small to absorb the summer population. Moving south, **Barbati Beach** has no real village, simply a trio of tavernas kept busy by the occupants of summer apartments available for rent. Behind the beach, villas are springing up, joining the clusters of development evident all the way north to Kassiopi.

To the south, **Pirgi** and **Ipsos** blend as one in a major apartment and villa development that has the singular disadvantage of being separated from the narrow pebble beach by an extremely busy road. Ipsos is also notorious for noisy late-night package-tour boat parties, whose music echoes relentlessly across the water until dawn. **Dassia**, dominated by large hotels, has an equally narrow beach, made all the more claustrophobic by the proximity of a row of slightly seedy tavernas and the looming presence of two hotels. **Gouvia**, a congested resort six miles north of Corfu town in a sheltered but noisy bay, has splendid scenery, unlimited watersports and two dynamic discos. The route back into the capital is completed by passing **Kontokali**, another package-tour resort that the discriminating traveller may find brash and insensitive.

Getting there

By air direct from Gatwick, Luton, Stansted (3¼ hours); Bristol, Birmingham, Cardiff, East Midlands (3½ hours); Leeds, Manchester, Newcastle (3¾ hours); Belfast, Glasgow (4 hours). There are several flights daily between Athens and Corfu (45 minutes). Kerkyra airport is one mile south of Corfu town.

By bus and ferry on an inclusive ticket from Athens to Corfu town (11 hours).

By Motorail from Boulogne to Bologna or Paris to Rimini, leaving a fast route down the Adriatic coast. By driving to almost the toe of Italy, Corfu is accessible from Brindisi by car ferry, a sea journey of eight hours. Many ferries stop at Corfu *en route* between Italy and various eastern Mediterranean ports.

Local transport

The bus service on Corfu is cheap and reliable, but does not yet extend to the more remote resorts, especially in the south-west. Corfu has been waging a campaign against fare dodgers, so keep your ticket: inspectors carry out frequent checks. Hiring a car is expensive and can be frustrating, as very few of the roads on the island encourage speed. They have not been engineered to allow easy navigation of the bends, and at any point you may be confronted with a stationary cart or animal. Casualties among moped-users are extremely high because of the number of unpredictable pot-holes.

Weather

Averages	Jan	Feb	Mar	Apr	May	Jun
Temperature	50	50	54	59	66	75
Sun hours	5	6	7	7	9	10
Rainy days	13	9	8	6	4	2
Sea temp.	59	59	59	61	64	70

Averages	Jul	Aug	Sep	Oct	Nov	Dec
Temperature	81	79	73	66	59	54
Sun hours	11	12	9	6	4	3
Rainy days	1	2	4	10	12	17
Sea temp.	75	77	75	70	66	64

In high season rain is only a remote possibility and the temperature is not oppressively hot. June and late September are the ideal months to visit Corfu. December is by far the wettest month, January the coldest.

Crete

The largest island in Greece, Crete offers a rare
combination of outstanding sightseeing and sustained
sunshine. Its turbulent past can be traced back more than
4000 years to the Minoans, named after the legendary
King Minos. The Minoan civilisation flourished from about
2600BC to 1450BC, when an unknown disaster – perhaps
the volcanic eruption on Santorini or an enemy attack –
destroyed it. Later, the Venetians, the Turks and the
Germans in turn each seized Crete by force, but without
ever subduing its people, who continued to resist from the
wild hinterland, a backbone of three formidable mountain
ranges interspersed with dangerous gorges and ravines.
This history of fierce independence gives Crete a unique
identity that it is eager to share.

Crete has not become entirely subordinated to tourism,
important though this industry is to its economy. The
island is intensely cultivated, producing 15 per cent of all
Greek wine, 25 per cent of Greek olive oil and 90 per cent
of the Greek currant crop. Life goes on largely unspoilt and
unaffected by the influx of holiday-makers, especially in
the inland villages. Here, the men still wear tall boots and
baggy trousers kept up by ancient cartridge belts, with the
odd knife or two tucked in for good measure. Festivals are
staged not for the benefit of tourists but for the villagers
themselves. Almost everyone wears national dress. At
weddings, expect to see a little orchestra, providing
beautiful exotic music on flute and lyre. Throughout the
year sunset marks for every village the time of the *volta*,
the evening stroll.

Even at the very height of summer you can always find a
place at which to stay anywhere outside the main resorts if
you choose to do any touring. It may consist only of a
simple room, but there will be a taverna or two, a friendly
if slightly over-curious local population, and a bus to take
you back to your apartment.

Crete has a wide variety of self-catering accommodation,
ranging from rooms and spartan apartments to modest

CRETE

villas and, unusual for Greece, bungalows that form part of a hotel complex and offer many of the advantages of self-catering (such as privacy and independence) with fewer disadvantages (such as washing up). These bungalows can be found in particular on the north-east coast just outside **Agios Nikolaos**, the largest and most crowded resort in Crete, 43 miles (1 hour 15 minutes) from the airport at Heraklion.

Named after the saint whose church of St Nicholas is near the harbour, Agios Nikolaos has altered unimaginably since its days as a peaceful little fishing port. Its principal attraction is the so-called Lake Voulismeni, a deep inner harbour joined to the outer harbour by a narrow canal. Most of the tavernas in this area provide accommodation, though the better the view, the higher their prices, especially along the sea-front to the north of the harbour. For visitors without children, the rather shabby backstreets have a vibrant nightlife, too vibrant perhaps for those who elect to sleep there. Cafés and bars, many with music and dancing, stay open until nearly dawn, and so do several extremely noisy discos. The cognoscenti seem to congregate at Rocky's, Scorpio and The Studio.

Agios Nikolaos is not the place for a beach holiday. Visitors have to settle for concrete bathing-platforms, put down between the rocks, and two narrow beaches that are little more than strips of shingle. The nearest sandy beach, near the Dolphin Taverna on the promenade two miles to the north, is impossibly crowded in midsummer, although it does offer a great many water activities, including pedalos, snorkelling, waterskiing and windsurfing.

Of the hotel/bungalow complexes, the best is **Minos Beach** , two miles outside the town, with a hundred bungalows set in lovely gardens that lead direct to a cove of rock and sand. Its large swimming-pool is particularly attractive, and the restaurant is recommended. **Mirabello**, also two miles from Agios, has 128 bungalows (open in the summer only) and two swimming-pools, one set aside for children, who can also have separate meals. The nearest beach, a mixture of rock and pebble, is across the busy main road, and at the adult pool there is an irritating charge for sunbeds.

Hera Village, three miles north of the resort, consists entirely of 44 bungalows, built into the hillside, with an outstanding view across the bay. It has a large swimming-pool, a separate children's pool, and an evening disco. Each level of the complex involves steps or ramps and an awkward climb down to the shingle beach.

Each of these complexes can be booked as part of a package tour, and all have good connections to Agios Nikolaos. Their willingness to take bookings without main meals seems to depend on the take-up of space by major tour companies. Self-catering visitors should note that most bungalows have only limited cooking facilities and that by staying on a room-only basis they may not automatically be entitled to use the free transport into Agios; the town does have an excellent bus service, though.

South-east of Agios, little groups of villas, linked by rough tracks, have been built between the hillside village of **Kalo Chorio** and the sea, where the beaches are less crowded and slightly superior – part sand, part pebble. Further east, the beach closest to the Minoan settlement of **Gournia** is polluted. Try instead **Pahia Ammos**, which has a clean beach and agreeable rooms, with limited cooking facilities, to rent in the village.

As the Gulf of Mirabello gives way to the open sea, the coast becomes hazardous for swimming and is buffeted by fierce waves. Bathing is not really safe until you reach the north-east town of **Sitia**, whose beach of grey coarse sand is less appealing than its high terraces of little white houses. Other than basic rooms, self-catering accommodation here is in short supply, but the seaside restaurants are good value. Beyond Sitia the road forks east to **Palaikastro**, a bustling village whose women greet the tourists off the bus, inviting them to inspect their rooms. A rough track leads down to a sandy, undeveloped beach, practically deserted for much of the year, which is more than can be said for the palm beach at **Vai**, just to the north, which, though wide, is awash with visitors. The main road, such as it is, leads through an eerie valley of jagged rock to **Kato Zakros**, site of a Minoan palace (plenty to see, even though the excavations are still continuing). Tourists for whom creature comforts are a low priority can stay in self-catering rooms just off the pebble beach, run by two tavernas whose regular clientele remain a mystery in this remote spot.

Beyond Zakros, road and settlements simply cease to exist, and you have to retrace your steps to Sitia before striking south. Here, visitors have the benefit of subdued seas and balmy breezes from North Africa, although the beaches are still of grey sand. One of the safest for children, gently shelving seemingly for miles, is at **Makriyialos**, where the road from the north reaches the south coast. Major development is expected here. The nearby cove just west of **Kolimbos**, which also has a new villa development, is among the more agreeable locations on the island. Just to the west, **Ferma** also has isolated villas but it is too close to the industrial centre of **Ierapetra**, whose long grey aspect is all too synonymous with the sprawling grey town. It is, however, expanding rapidly as a tourist resort, with an adequate beach and a sea-front jammed end to end with tavernas and discos. **Arvi** has a much better beach, the first of a string of little communities reached by unlinked bumpy roads. Next comes **Keratokambos**, just to the west, an attractive and largely unspoilt seaside village. **Matala** was once the centre of a huge hippie colony, who became temporary troglodytes in its caves. The summer population is still very young, the village over-commercial and relatively expensive, a reflection of its proximity to the Minoan ruins at Komo. Matala's beach is extremely crowded in mid-summer.

Moving west, a long ribbon of greyish sand stretches to **Agia Galini**, the only major package-tour resort on the south coast, reached by a sinuous road between sheer cliffs, ripe for ambush in the days of Cretan banditry. Now you are much more likely to be parted from your money by harbour-side cafés and discos, whose prices are high. A large number of young people congregate in this fashionable resort during the summer, and they are less likely to be deterred by the principal disadvantage of the accommodation, most of which is located up a very steep hill some way from the beach. But there are a few rooms near the sea, run by local hotels as a panacea for indignant over-booked package tourists. Agia Galini's sea-front is extremely congested at the height of the season, but around the headland lies a sequence of shingle coves, each successively less crowded than the last. The town is a convenient base from which to visit most parts of the island. The important Minoan palaces at Phaistos and Agia Triada are nearby.

The road west goes inland again, through the village of **Spili**, which has basic accommodation and where you can be lulled off to sleep by the sound of its cascading fountains. Detour south to the **Preveli Monastery**, a focal-point of Cretan resistance to the Nazis, which has rooms but no cooking facilities.

The main road, such as it is, rejoins the south coast just short of **Plakias**, whose original fishing village has been ruined by a haphazard, poorly constructed villa and apartment development. Plakias offers three beaches, each of grey sand and small stones, including picturesque coves on each side of the resort.

The Gorge of Samaria, probably the longest in Europe, is a superb four- or five-hour walking excursion through spectacular scenery. Reached by bus or car via the road from the north coast between Chania and Omalos, it also bisects the western end of Crete. The sheer weight of tourists – many thousands a day in summer – has ruined the settlements of **Agia Roumeli**, at the exit to the gorge, and **Hora Sfakion**, linked to the gorge by motor-boats (about 1 hour 30 minutes) and to Chania by early-evening bus. However, most of the boats call *en route* at the remote yet delightful village of **Loutro**, which by accident therefore has the benefit of quite exceptional transport links for a few hours each day. So far, Loutro, which has basic accommodation and a lively if eccentric taverna, receives few visitors, many no doubt deterred by the hazardous mountain road west of Hora Sfakion. East of Hora lies the ruined Venetian fort of Frangokastello, below which is a broad sandy beach with a taverna.

Because of the gorge, the remaining south- and west-coast villages can be reached only through Chania in the north, and even then on separate, largely indifferent roads spreading out from Chania like a giant's fingers. The most accessible, the south-coast resort of **Paleohora**, has a sweeping, sandy bay backed by trees, and is highly popular with campers. There have been complaints about some of its more permanent accommodation, on which investment has been skimpy. The village is extremely friendly, and half its houses are turned into makeshift tavernas for the summer season, making the main street one huge outdoor restaurant. There are two noisy discos. From Paleohora boats travel twice a week to the tiny island of **Gavdos**, the southernmost point of Europe and supposed to be the home of the nymph Calypsos, whose charms kept Odysseus diverted for eight years. Gavdos has basic rooms, but visitors should note that the boats are frequently cancelled in rough weather.

On the desolate west coast of Crete itself, **Kambos** has simple accommodation, but the road here is extremely rough in places. **Sfinario**, more accessible, also has a few rooms close to a pebble beach. Moving north, the ruined city of **Falassarna** overlooks a beautifully clear, sandy beach; the nearby taverna rents rooms.

Some of the north-west coast runs into marshland, with stretches of tall reeds that make bathing hazardous and are a breeding-ground for insects. Avoid **Kastelli Kissamou**, the most westerly town, whose beach consists mainly of rocks and is extremely grubby. Moving east, **Maleme** has a grey sand beach marred by some sharp pebbles and rather over-patronised by holiday-makers escaping the clutches of a nearby large (and loud) hotel. **Agia Marina's** sandy beach is a much more attractive colour, and the bay, safe and quiet, is ideal for families with small children. But its days may be numbered by the steady villa and apartment development (much of it separated from the sea by a busy main road) making its way steadily eastwards to the next village, **Platanias**.

Immediately east is **Chania**, the second largest town in Crete, with its own international airport. Despite its vibrant market-place, the commercial centre is rather ugly, and sailors from the nearby naval base of Souda Bay are much in evidence. But the narrow lanes leading to the original Venetian harbour and its old quarter are hugely attractive. In the evening the main, outer harbour is closed to traffic, leaving visitors to stroll undisturbed among its colourful lines of bars and restaurants on the quayside. Chania's beaches, a series of four bays west of the town, are a bus-ride away, and there is very little self-catering accommodation nearby.

Proceeding east, **Georgiopoulis** is a sleepy village off the tourist track renting pleasant rooms, with a wide but safe, shallow river running through its sandy beach into the sea.

The next town, **Rethymnon**, is slightly smaller than Chania, and much more picturesque. It has a mixture of Turkish and Venetian architecture, with churches and minarets, and houses with wooden balconies, all crammed together in climbing streets. A few rooms are available close to the Venetian harbour, but most of the self-catering accommodation is at the back of the town, some way from the splendid, sandy beach.

This stretch of fine beaches continues through the villages of **Stavromenos** and **Panormos**, with expanding tourist development; but once again many of the self-catering villas and apartments are separated from the shore by a fast and dangerous road. Only **Bali**, a little village in its own rocky cove, escapes the worst of the traffic, and it has only rooms to rent. Some of the accommodation in **Agia Pelagia**, located at the end of a sinuous road in the very centre of the north coast, is set back from the village and reached only by a stiff uphill walk. However, if you can find accommodation down in the bay near the sandy beach, the view is superb and all the shops and restaurants are close by.

Further east, **Linoperamata** and **Ammoudara** are fast-developing resorts with some self-catering accommodation. Their safe, sandy beaches do not compensate for uninspired surroundings, including an oil refinery right by the sea.

Nearby **Heraklion**, Crete's capital, is ugly, frenetic and without a single beach. It is of value only as a disembarkation point or a lunch stop on the way to the Archaeological Museum or the ruins of **Knossos** to the south. This partial re-creation of a great Minoan palace, which 4000 years ago had flushing lavatories and hot and cold running water, is controversial and can be confusing, but no holiday on Crete would be complete without a visit.

East of Heraklion, aircraft noise is particularly severe at **Amnissos**, right on the flightpath of the international airport. The sandy beach here is often strewn with litter, left by day-trippers from Heraklion. The next resort, **Kokkini Hani**, also suffers from aircraft noise. **Gournes** is close to a NATO military base but is also conveniently placed for trips on to the Lasithi Plateau, including the Diktaian Cave, legendary birthplace of Zeus. Three of the villages on the plateau, Agios Georgios, Psichro and Tzermiadon, have simple accommodation.

Back on the coast, **Hersonisos**, once a Roman spa, is much more attractive, particularly for visitors looking for a resort with plenty of activities. Its lively sea-front overlooks a narrow sandy beach, which is much less crowded where it widens beyond the headland. Self-catering accommodation in the town suffers from disco noise, and villas and apartments on the outskirts are separated from the sea by a busy road.

The next resort, **Stalis**, has a gently sloping sandy beach but little else to offer. **Malia**, a victim of its own success, has ruined the atmosphere of its original village and its narrow winding streets by allowing a random development down to the sea. The main tourist area is beset by through traffic on a dangerous road, and much of the accommodation is on the wrong side for access to the sandy beach. Just beyond lies **Sisi**, a quiet village resort, with charming sandy coves.

Elounda, the last significant resort before Agios Nikolaos, is rapidly expanding and may soon lose its relaxed atmosphere. The exceptional scenery and charm of its small fishing harbour may also be insufficient compensation for the mediocre beaches close by, mainly man-made concrete and rock platforms built by the large hotels. On the headland north towards the village of **Plaka**, villas and apartments are closer to more satisfactory beaches of coarse sand. The whole area has exceptionally good sports facilities, especially sailing and scuba-diving.

Getting there

By air direct to Heraklion or Chania from Gatwick, Luton (4 hours); Birmingham, Bristol, East Midlands (4¼ hours); Manchester, Newcastle (4½ hours); Glasgow (4¾ hours). Up to seven flights daily from Athens to Heraklion, up to four to Chania (both 45 minutes). Some Chania flights continue to Rethymnon. Heraklion airport is two miles east of the capital, at the centre of the north coast, while Chania airport, nine miles east of the town, is in the far west and may be less suitable for transfers to other parts of the island.

By boat from Piraeus, daily, to Souda Bay (for Chania, at least 12 hours), Heraklion (12 hours), Agios Nikolaos (14 hours) and Sitia (15 hours). Twice-weekly sailings from Piraeus to Kastelli via the Peloponnese.

Local transport

Car rental is expensive on Crete, and many of the prices initially quoted for car hire may not include full insurance and local taxes. Some cars offered by smaller firms are in poor condition and should be checked carefully. Missing jacks and spare tyres are common, an important consideration in view of the fact that the inland roads are extremely pot-holed. For much the same reason, some insurance cover arranged in the UK specifically excludes damage to the underside of the vehicle. A car is essential for reaching many of the more remote beaches and villages. Many roads are poorly signposted.

The hiring of mopeds is not recommended as they are rarely covered fully by insurance, and crash helmets are scarcely ever provided.

The main bus terminals are at Heraklion, Chania and Agios Nikolaos, and sightseeing by bus should be planned via one of these centres. Buses are cheap and reliable, with services starting around 6.30 a.m. Few buses run later than 7.30 p.m. outside the main resorts.

Weather

Averages	Jan	Feb	Mar	Apr	May	Jun
Temperature	60	60	64	70	76	82
Sun hours	5	6	6	8	9	12
Rainy days	11	10	5	3	2	1
Sea temp.	61	61	63	64	68	73

Averages	Jul	Aug	Sep	Oct	Nov	Dec
Temperature	86	86	82	78	70	66
Sun hours	13	12	10	7	6	6
Rainy days	0	0	1	4	6	11
Sea temp.	75	77	75	73	66	63

In summer inland temperatures can rise above 100°F in early afternoon, making energetic activity extremely difficult. July and August (when the *meltemi* wind is particularly fierce) have practically guaranteed sunshine. Winters in Crete, though mild, are rather wet; the south coast is both drier and milder than the north.

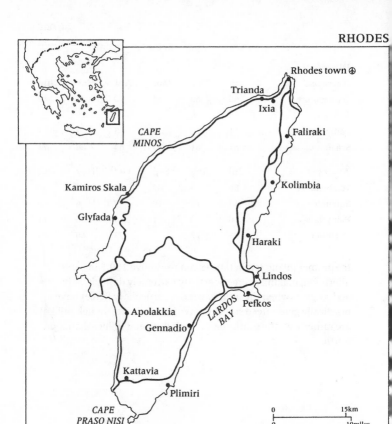

Rhodes

The sunniest climate in Greece, some superb beaches and a history stretching back beyond the time of Helen of Troy ensure that Rhodes has something to offer every visitor. There are, though, a great many of them: half a million or more, mainly crammed into the summer season from the end of April to the end of September. Although Rhodes is a traditional package-tour destination, with many large hotels, it offers a wide range of self-catering accommodation, including large villas, flats and hundreds of simple rooms in seaside villages.

The self-catering capital of Rome is **Lindos**, at one time a delightful fishing village. It has an early acropolis and was visited by the Apostle Paul. Modern, reconstructed Lindos, a dazzling white landmark on the east coast of the island, is entirely devoted to the requirements of the self-catering tourist, as it has no hotels – the nearest are on Vliha Bay, three miles north. The winding main street of Lindos is crammed with tavernas offering all-day bacon and eggs. Unlike many Greek islands, however, the sheer turnover of both customers and staff renders the service brusque and incompetent. Accommodation ranges from sparse, tiny rooms to smart houses, but those near the traffic-free main street suffer from considerable noise, especially late at night when the discos reach a rare pitch of excitement. The most agreeable accommodation has a shaded, central courtyard, a great asset in the extreme summer heat. Some of the best apartments offer fine views of Lindos Bay and lie midway to the beach, a steep climb that young children may find difficult. Lindos Bay is sandy and safe, but, like the rest of Lindos, touches saturation point at the height of the season. Only watersport enthusiasts find that the facilities outweigh the frenzy. You can escape the crowds by going to the adjacent Bay of St Paul, but swimming here is entirely from rocks, and for much of the day it is shaded from the sun by a sheer cliff-face. The beautiful acropolis, above the town, has fourth- and fifth-century temples; it is best seen soon after dawn, before the tourists arrive by bus and donkey. Lindos is too spectacular a spot to be dismissed as a resort, but it is an experience for which visitors must literally pay a high price – the highest on the island.

South of Lindos, **Pefkos** is a much quieter village on the edge of Lardos Bay, with a narrow beach of slightly coarse sand set against splendid scenery. Although the facilities are improving, there are no hotels and this is not the place for visitors unable to amuse themselves, especially at night. Much of the self-catering accommodation is new and, by Greek standards, well appointed – which is more than can be said for some of the tracks leading to the villas, both unmade and unlit.

Gennadio, best reached on the old coast road from Lardos, is ideally placed to take advantage of the unspoilt beaches, a mixture of sand and small pebbles, in the south-east corner of the island beyond Lardos Bay. Gennadio itself is uninspired and isolated, and offers only the most modest accommodation – as does the curved bay of **Plimiri**, once a holiday resort for occupying Italian forces but now virtually abandoned except for a restaurant in splendid isolation.

The main road from Lardos turns inland to Kattavia, from where a rough track leads to Cape Praso Nisi, whose twin strips of sand, virtually deserted except at the very height of summer, are probably the best beaches on the island.

The sand-dunes of the south-west corner in the long bay beneath the hillside village of **Apolakkia** have even fewer visitors, largely because they are exposed to the wind, and have a rough sea and strong currents, a disadvantage of the entire western shore. **Glyfada** is an emerging resort, but its beach, like much of this coast, consists largely of pebble and rock. The same is true of **Kamiros Skala**, a thriving little fishing village noted for its lively taverna. There is some sand at **Cape Minos**, close to the outstanding archaeological site of the ancient ruined city of Kamiros, whose streets date from the third century BC.

The north-west corner between **Ixia** and **Trianda** has a number of particular disadvantages. Both settlements suffer severely from traffic noise on the coast road between Rhodes town and the airport, and the road separates many of the self-catering apartment blocks from the beach, so crossing it can be hazardous for families. Trianda has the added handicap of lying directly on the flightpath to Rhodes airport. The pebble beach at Ixia is particularly crowded in midsummer with people staying at the large hotels and apartment blocks here.

Rhodes town, on the northernmost tip of the island, is essentially a package-tour hotel destination, with relatively little self-catering accommodation. Its beaches are windy and hugely overcrowded. The New Town, full of large hotels, is extremely noisy at night because of its discos and two-wheeled traffic. But there are agreeable parts in which to stay, especially close to Mandraki Harbour with its arcaded shops and cafés.

From this harbour eight Rhodean ships set sail to join the thousand launched to bring back Queen Helen from the Trojans. Nearby, though not spanning its entrance, stood the Colossus of Rhodes, a 100-foot-high bronze statue numbered among the Seven Wonders of the Ancient World. Wrecked by an earthquake in 226BC, it lay in pieces for 900 years until it was carted off to Syria and sold as scrap.

In the Middle Ages the island became the home of the Knights Hospitallers of St John, a body of knights committed to preventing the Muslim Turks from dominating the Mediterranean. Lying just 12 miles from Asia, Rhodes had always been an easy prey for Turkish invaders. The Knights fortified the capital and continued to defend the island for 200 years. The battlemented walls of the Old Town enclose the great Palace of the Grand Masters, the Hospital of the Knights, and the Street of the Knights that leads in turn into a maze of alleys containing a Turkish bazaar and a genuine Turkish bath.

The Old Town also has the best restaurants on Rhodes, with fish specialities much cheaper than elsewhere in the Greek islands. Wine is produced locally by the Compagnie Agricole et Industrièlle de Rhodes (CAIR), including a quite palatable *retsina*, the fine white Rhodos and Lindos, and Chevalier du Rhodes, a strong dry red.

South of Rhodes town, the east-coast resort of **Faliraki** has safe bathing from an unappetising beach of grey sand. The original village has been swallowed up by a major construction programme involving both large hotels and self-catering accommodation. The centre of the complex is extremely noisy, and some apartments are separated from the beach by the main road, which is both busy and dangerous. The best area to stay in is close to a smaller sandy beach to the south, tree-lined, sheltered but unfortunately very crowded.

Off the road south to Lindos, **Kolimbia** has a number of villas to rent among the plane trees. But they are a long walk from the two sand and pebble bays at Cape Vagia, where the sea floods spectacularly into a smooth crater of sandstone. The quiet fishing village of **Haraki**, beneath the ruined castle of Feraklos, offers rooms overlooking a bay of grey sand and pebble.

Getting there

By air direct from Gatwick, Luton (4 hours); Birmingham, Cardiff, East Midlands (4¼ hours); Manchester, Newcastle (4½ hours). Up to four flights daily from Athens (55 minutes). Rhodes airport is 25 minutes from the centre of Rhodes town.

By boat from Piraeus, four or five times a week, via the Cyclades or Dodecanese Islands (of which Rhodes is the major island). The journey takes a minimum of 18 hours.

Local transport

Car hire is expensive, and local car rental firms may be underinsured for personal accident purposes. All cars should be inspected carefully for mechanical defects, and each tyre examined, including the spare. Some insurance cover arranged in the UK specifically excludes damage to the underside of the car and to the tyres, an indication of the poor quality of many of the roads. Unfortunately, some of the roughest mountain routes, such as from Kattavia to Apolakkia, are also among the most rewarding. A car is essential to reach many of the more remote beaches and villages. If you travel very early in the day you will avoid the masses of tourist coaches that descend on the island's beauty-spots, such as the Valley of the Butterflies at Petaloudes, not far from the airport. Buy a good map, as many of the roads are very badly signposted.

Hiring a taxi for a whole day may be as cheap as a hire car. Prices to regular tourist destinations are fixed, but it is prudent to agree the fare in advance.

Local buses go to all the major resorts, though less regularly to Pefkos. The buses are extremely cheap and surprisingly reliable, but incredibly crowded from lunchtime onwards. Services south of Lindos operate only very early in the morning or late in the evening.

Weather

Averages	Jan	Feb	Mar	Apr	May	Jun
Temperature	54	54	55	63	70	77
Sun hours	4	5	7	8	10	14
Rainy days	15	10	8	4	4	1
Sea temp.	59	57	59	63	66	72

Averages	Jul	Aug	Sep	Oct	Nov	Dec
Temperature	81	82	78	68	61	55
Sun hours	14	13	11	8	5	4
Rainy days	0	0	1	6	8	13
Sea temp.	75	77	75	73	66	61

Rhodes has long sunny periods between May and September, with negligible rainfall in July and August, when, however, the *meltemi* wind blows relentlessly from the north. Inland temperatures are uncomfortably high in the summer months. Between November and March a different Rhodes emerges: cold and disagreeably wet.

Italy

Contrary to the popular misconception that the travel
industry in Italy revolves around British, German and
Swedish visitors, the statistics show clearly that it still
depends primarily on its domestic market. By and large
Italians choose not to go abroad for their summer holidays
(the weakness of the lira may have something to do with
it); instead, they return year after year to the vast numbers
of small family hotels – generally by the sea, as three-
quarters of all Italians prefer to take their holidays on the
coast. The British package tourist is often left with a choice
between purpose-built hotels in largely artificial resorts
and a sprinkling of up-market establishments in such
fashionable and expensive places as Venice and San Remo.

Fortunately, self-catering restores the balance. Few
Italians are enthusiasts for holidays where they have to
make their own beds and buy and cook their own food. So
the field is left clear for foreigners who have these eccentric
inclinations. Just about every barn, cottage, bungalow,
farmhouse, villa, apartment and castle that could
conceivably be defined as a holiday let is placed on the
market each summer.

Many properties are part of a network – of agents, sub-
agents and go-betweens – whose complexity is designed to
frustrate the Italian tax collector, but which makes it
equally difficult for a visitor ever to complain to the real
owner. The problem is compounded by the absence in Italy
of a proper equivalent of the French *gîte* system (see page

9), despite the huge number of farmhouses interested in offering accommodation – an estimated 150,000 in Tuscany alone. Some property owners in Tuscany and Umbria take part in the embryonic *agriturismo* organisation, offering self-contained apartments on farms with the option of farmhouse breakfasts. It is operated by Agriturist (Piazza S. Firenze 3, 50122 Firenze (Florence), telephone 010-39-55287838, for Tuscany; Via Tuderte 30, 06100 Perugia, telephone 010-39-7530174, for Umbria). However, printed information is published only in Italian, and making reservations requires perseverance and usually some knowledge of the language.

In rural areas, especially in the south, several local families sometimes club together to furnish a house for the summer; the furnishings are what the average British holiday-maker would regard as sparse, although the locals would see them as luxurious. However, many properties in popular tourist areas are beyond reproach – superbly appointed, with swimming-pools and maid service, and at prices far below the equivalent on the French Riviera. Italy also has an increasingly large selection of what might be termed 'holiday villages', flats and chalets in a self-contained complex with its own shops and restaurants, usually beside a beach or lake, with private bathing facilities and water-sports.

As inland Italy can be very hot in midsummer, and swimming-pools remain the exception rather than the norm, beaches are often central to a successful self-catering holiday. Apart from treating with scepticism brochures' claims concerning its proximity to the property, visitors should realise that the beach is, for the Italians, another avenue to profit: with the notable exception of Lido di Jesolo, north of Venice, practically every worthwhile beach on the Italian mainland is run by self-styled and often self-appointed concessionaires. In return for keeping the beach clear of rubbish, they are allowed to charge for umbrellas, sunbeds, deckchairs and cabins. Even if your self-catering holiday is part of a package, it is extremely rare for it to include beach charges. In the more fashionable resorts, these charges can be positively extortionate, so much so that on the Venice Lido one British visitor, on hearing the weekly hire charge of a beach chalet, believed that he was being quoted the purchase price.

However, under Italian law the five metres between the high-tide mark and the sea are public property, so tourists with nerves of steel can enter a private beach, decline to pay, and set up their own deckchairs right at the front. For those with less courage a public section of the beach can usually be found a little distance away, but it will have very few facilities.

Price is one problem: pollution is another. The beaches close to the major ports of Genoa, La Spezia, Naples, Salerno, Taranto, Palermo, Ancona and Venice all have traces of oil and sewage. Long stretches of the Adriatic have been marred by slicks of brownish slime which, even when apparently eradicated, reconstitute themselves just below the surface.

What to take with you

Your route to Italy must influence what you take. If you are travelling by air or rail, you have little choice but to keep your luggage to a minimum, so many of the items recommended below may be ruled out on grounds of size or weight. But if you are travelling by car, it is relatively simple to overcome the traditional shortcomings of a holiday home.

With the exception of a few luxury villas or those owned by the British, self-catering accommodation in Italy is practically certain not to include a kettle, a teapot, a food processor, a cheese grater, a whisk, a peppermill or an egg-cup. As many of the properties are particularly remote, or in villages without the Italian equivalent of a corner shop, it is also prudent to assume that other, more essential items may also not be immediately available: these can include a bottle-opener, tin-opener, corkscrew, matches, refuse bags and a sharp kitchen knife. Also likely to prove useful are a pair of pliers for emergency repairs, a small adjustable spanner for connecting cooking-gas bottles, a torch with new batteries and a set of small screwdrivers with a single changeable handle.

Take an adaptor, or some standard Continental two-pin plugs, for use with a hair-drier or electric razor. Most of Italy has the same 220-volt AC supply as Britain, but a few remote villages use 115–125 volts DC, which is unsuitable for many UK electrical items. Some larger towns and cities possess both voltages, sometimes even in the same house, which can be particularly confusing.

Italians like buying in bulk, which is fine if you are a permanent resident but extremely wasteful on a fortnight's holiday. Expect to be offered large packs of soap powder, washing-up liquid, dishwasher powder, sugar and salt. Unless you are happy to make a generous offering of the unused portions to the people staying at the property after you, consider taking a selection of common items from the UK in small plastic containers.

Although the price gap is narrowing, instant coffee and well-known brands of tea-bags are more expensive in Italy than they are in the UK, so you may prefer to take your own. Concentrated drinks that need to be diluted, such as orange or lemon squash, are virtually unknown even in quite large towns. British breakfast cereal is generally available but is expensive. Camera film is cheaper in the UK, and while film processing can be cheaper in Italy it is also much less reliable.

Eating in

Italians take eating very seriously: some 40 per cent of their disposable income is spent on food.

The word supermarket (*supermercato*) is used to describe general stores of all shapes and sizes. They are often open when other shops are closed, and they are a particularly useful source of packed and frozen foods, including many varieties of pasta. Many Italian supermarkets will deliver to your villa or apartment for no extra charge – ask at the check-out before you shop.

The market (*mercato*) is a traditional feature of Italian food shopping. In smaller towns and villages the market may be open from early morning until noon on one day a week, in larger towns every day except Sunday. All markets sell fresh fruit and vegetables, each stall usually having its own speciality; some offer meat and poultry, too, usually in a separate covered area to shield the produce from the sun. In seaside towns there may be a separate fish market near the port. Larger markets also have a variety of non-food products that seem cheap, though generally the quality of such items is poor. Local shoppers rarely have a list of items they want to buy and simply choose what takes their fancy on the day.

Greengrocers (*verdolerie*) are generally found only in cities. Traditionally, customers take one of the baskets provided, help themselves to fruit and vegetables and take them inside to be weighed. A fruiterer (*fruttivendolo*) will often sell vegetables as well as fruit. Everything is sold by the kilogramme unless marked *l'uno*. The lack of choice is often conspicuous.

Butchers (*macellerie*) sell both meat and poultry. In the north of Italy, beef products, especially veal, are good value; in the south, lamb. Italian cuts differ only slightly from those in Britain and, as in the UK, joints are tied up for roasting. Chicken is either sold whole with innards (it is rarely gutted) or in pieces. Some shops (*rosticcerie;* see also Eating Out) have a spit and offer ready-cooked meals, including roast meats and pasta.

Fishmongers (*pescherie*) are comparatively rare because most fish is bought at market. The chances are that at the fishmonger fish sold as fresh will in fact have been frozen and then thawed.

Bakeries (*panetteria* or *panificio*) no longer confine themselves to their own products baked on the premises, although many specialise in home-made pizzas and pastries. Their standard bread (*pane*) is sometimes called 'Tipo O' (the name of a particular quality of flour). A speciality is *focaccia*, bread soaked in olive oil and seasoned. For *croissants* you may have to call in at a local coffee shop (see below).

Italy makes the best ice-cream in the world, with imaginative varieties, and no visit would be complete without trying some. Many ice-cream parlours (*gelaterie*) are combined with a cake shop (*pasticceria*). Elaborate cakes and sweets are part of the staple diet, but they are certainly not cheap.

The delicatessen (*salumeria* or *alimentari*) specialises in pasta sauces, hams, salamis, sausages and a variety of pre-cooked fresh meals. *Alimentari* is also used as the grandiose name for a corner shop, stocking a little of everything, usually beaten on price but rarely on character.

Eating out

There are a great many restaurants in Italy, but very few non-Italian ones. The Italians like their own national cuisine, and, apart from a few in major cities, foreign restaurants are practically unknown.

Italian restaurants and snack bars will be one of the following types. The *paninoteca* (from the Italian for filled rolls, *panini*) is a kind of sandwich bar-cum-coffee shop, specialising in toasted sandwiches. The actual bar may not have seats but will often serve an adjacent terrace. *Caffe* is a coffee shop, open from very early in the morning until late at night for all kinds of drinks as well as coffee, sandwiches, *croissants*, cakes and pastries. Breakfast here is particularly good value. The coffee shop has seats, but you can halve the price by paying the cashier in advance, putting in your order and consuming your food or drink standing at the counter.

The *tavola calda* is a self-service restaurant, usually offering a selection of hot dishes, which is cheaper than most other restaurants except in tourist centres, where they can be grotesquely overpriced.

Rosticcerie specialise in meat or poultry roasted on a spit, though they may also serve traditional pasta dishes. Where they have somewhere to sit down, it will often be extremely rough and ready.

The *locanda* is a simple, local, country restaurant, family-run, serving local dishes, and offering only a very limited choice. It is likely to be extremely good value. An *osteria* was originally a rustic inn specialising in home cooking, though it is now much less predictable than that. Some *osterie* are extremely fashionable and expensive, however remote. The emphasis in most of them tends to be on the wine (served by the carafe) rather than the food.

A *pizzeria* offers unsophisticated cooking, predominantly pizza and pasta, in humble surroundings – good vale for families. Most have an oven in public view so you can watch your pizza being prepared. Many *pizzerie* open only in the evenings.

Trattorie are less fashionable than restaurants and operate on slender margins, with the cooking and serving usually done by different members of the same family. If there is a menu, not every item listed will be available – it depends on what was bought at market.

Tablecloths and a sweets trolley are probably the most common distinguishing features of the more up-market *ristorante*, other than the bill. Some exhibit such a sense of occasion that they are worth the extra money, but some seem almost entirely patronised by tourists.

In general, restaurants offering no menu are likely to be the best value. Beware of those displaying a *menu turistico*, or a fixed-price menu, as it may be cunningly presented to disguise a number of extras, or you may be under some pressure once inside to choose other more expensive items than the normally dull and basic dishes on the tourist menu. There is sometimes a cover charge (*pane e coperto*) and a service charge (*servizio*) which together can add up to 25 per cent extra to your bill.

Lunch is the main meal in Italy and even in large cities it is traditional to allow as many workers as possible to go home for lunch. It will usually consist of *antipasto*, an hors d'oeuvre of cold meat; pasta; fish or meat, often with the vegetables (*contorni* or *verdure*) served separately; and finally dessert, fruit, cake or ice-cream. You need to sit down by 12.30 p.m. in a restaurant to be sure of a table, and you may have trouble being served if you enter after 2 p.m. Dinner is generally available between 7.30 and 9 p.m., slightly earlier in the countryside. Most restaurants close one day a week, often on Mondays. On Sundays and Bank Holidays it is essential to book a table for lunch.

Children

Italians love children: they are tolerated in hotels, shops and restaurants where in the UK they would be sent packing. Meals are scarcely a problem, because in almost every restaurant you can order pasta with a portion of chips (*patate fritte*) followed by ice-cream, which even the most discriminating child seems prepared to eat.

Baby food is readily available at *alimentari,* chemists (*farmacie*) and most supermarkets, although the brand names on jars and packets may be unfamiliar and the contents slightly different. The same shops stock disposable nappies, which are also on sale in certain clothes shops.

For babysitters, contact (and tip) the hall porter of any large hotel, irrespective of whether you are staying there. In villages you will find a queue of grandmothers ready and willing to look after small children, and you need have no reservation about your offspring's safety.

Transport

Every year the Italian government seems to hold a fierce debate on whether to offer petrol coupons and motorway toll vouchers to foreign motorists as an incentive to tourism. In the past a great many such vouchers seem to have found their way on to the black market. When the scheme is in operation (usually administered by the Automobile Association, the Royal Automobile Club and Citalia), its real value is significant only for visitors planning to drive to more remote destinations within Italy. This is more likely where motorists have already cut down their driving hours by taking a Motorail service from the Channel ports or Paris to Milan, Bologna or Rimini, which run regularly during the summer months.

Car hire is easy to arrange at most airports and main railway stations. However, combining it with a package deal bought in the UK is much more cost-effective, with savings of up to 50 per cent. Local dealers tend to charge similar prices to international companies, and are less conscientious in checking their vehicles. In Italy, where drivers tend to make the maximum use of the accelerator and the brake, collision damage waiver insurance is absolutely essential.

Train travel is much cheaper than it is in the UK, but faster services between major cities are subject to a compulsory supplement and seats often have to be reserved. Rover discount tickets are available to visitors for periods of up to two months.

Buses are cheap and reliable and operate throughout Italy. The principal hubs are Milan, Bologna, Rome and Naples, but every district has a network of local services. Many small companies operate both regular services and organised excursions, which tend to be cheaper than those run by larger companies catering exclusively for tourists. In small towns and villages, timetables are rarely provided at bus stops, and they are much more likely to be available in the post office, supermarket or chemist's.

Avoiding problems

In Italy, as in the UK, medicine is dispensed at the chemist's (*farmacia*) against a doctor's prescription. The pharmacist has a good deal more discretion than his British counterpart on what he may himself prescribe for minor ailments, including powerful drugs. To find a chemist's, look for a green or red cross on a white background.

Street crime is prolific in some tourist areas, especially by thieves operating on motor scooters, so keep a tight grip on your handbag or wallet and stay away from the kerb. Skilful pickpockets operate in all the major cities.

Female tourist are considered fair game by Italian men, first as an object of casual flirtation and then more seriously, given the slightest encouragement.

In any emergency, dial 113 anywhere in Italy and ask for *pronto soccorso* (immediate help).

Opening hours

In main towns, shops tend to open from 8.30 or 9 a.m. until 1 and then again from 4 until 8 p.m. From mid-June to mid-September, they often close on Saturday afternoons, reverting to closing on

Monday mornings for the rest of the year. Many food shops close all day on Wednesday but may be open on Sunday mornings. Most banks are open from 8.30 a.m. to 1.30 p.m. Monday to Friday.

Public holidays
1 January (New Year's Day); **6 January** (Epiphany); **Easter Monday; 25 April** (Liberation Day); **1 May** (Labour Day); **2 June** (Republic Day); **15 August** (*Ferragosto,* the Feast of the Assumption of the Virgin Mary); **1 November** *(Ognissanti,* All Saints' Day); **8 December** (Feast of the Immaculate Conception); **25 December** (Christmas Day); **26 December** (St Stephen's Day).

What to bring back
Shoes
Leather goods, including
   handbags and belts
Lace and embroidery
Glassware
Pottery
Perfume
Knitwear, especially sweaters
Cycling accessories
Model cars
Toy construction kits
T-shirts
Kitchen gadgets and utensils

Tour operators
For details see page 213

Allegro Holidays
Anglo-Italian Tourist Centre
Beach Villas
La Bella Toscana
Blakes Holidays
Bowhill Holidays
Bridgewater Villas
Casa Colonica
Chapter Travel
Citalia
City Cruiser Holidays
Continental Villas
CV Travel
Eurovillas
Ilios Island Holidays
Impact Holidays
Intasun Holidays
International Chapters
Invitation to Tuscany
Italian Interlude
Italian Tours
Just Italy
Lunigiana Holidays
Magic of Italy
Meon Travel
Newman, David
OSL
Patricia Wildblood
Pegasus Holidays
Perrymead Properties
Pleasurewood Holidays
Redwing Holidays
Seasun Tentrek
SFV Holidays
Traditional Tuscany
Tuscany from Cottages to
   Castles
Vacanze in Italia
Venetian Apartments
Villas Italia

TUSCANY

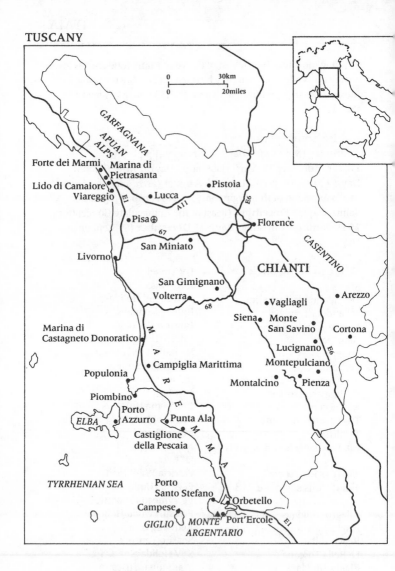

Tuscany

Only the rolling hills of Chianti country between the great
Renaissance cities of Florence and Siena represent the
Tuscany of popular imagination. The rest of the region
offers a series of dramatic contrasts. The long Tuscan coast
runs from the rugged foothills of the Apuan Alps, past the
Versilia, with its series of flat and uninspired resorts,
through a region of rocky, remote coves and beaches, to
the promontory of Argentario, a weekend retreat for the
sophisticated citizens of Rome. Inland is the Maremma, the
Camargue of Italy, complete with summer cowboys and
reclaimed marshes. North-east of Siena, beyond Arezzo,
are the chestnut-covered hills of the Casentino. North-
west of Florence lies the great Garfagnana, the infant
slopes of the Apennines, adding yet another dimension to
Tuscany.

If the countryside is far from uniform, the Tuscan
farmhouse has a timeless charm. Often rescued from some
medieval ruin, its weathered, terracotta walls, built on
brick foundations and supporting beamed ceilings, keep
the visitor cool in the fiercest heat. There are hundreds of
such houses, many with marvellous views across
vineyards and olive groves, either forming part of some
rustic village or a striking landmark in remote countryside.

Tuscan furniture, like the houses, is built to last. Oak and
pine are durable rather than elegant, and owners make
few concessions to comfort. They have, however,
recognised that villas with modern kitchens and
bathrooms command higher rents, and few are now
without proper amenities. But the plumbing and the
electricity rarely seem to match such improvements, so
blocked drains and blown fuses are common. Swimming-
pools, while not as widely available as they are in France or
Spain, are now a common feature. Pools are rarely filled
before early June and are usually emptied in late
September, and may even be left empty, or the water
changed infrequently, because of local shortages. If the
pool is a vital consideration, seek written assurance on its

condition from the owner, rental company or tour operator before you travel.

By no means all the best houses appear in brochures. Some owners prefer to advertise in British Sunday newspapers, relying on the draw of Tuscany to attract bookings. Although there are exceptions, in general there is little evidence that visitors save money by booking direct. Owners tend to maximise the price they can get for the summer season in the knowledge that they are less likely than companies to pick up off-peak bookings.

Indeed, if the owners live abroad, it may cost their clients more in postage and telephone calls to sort out a confirmed booking, and, if mistakes do occur, the clients' only remedy is to sue the owners direct – especially difficult where the owners are Italian nationals. Some owners appoint a part-time agent in the UK to handle bookings. While this may cut the cost of making the arrangements, potential visitors should bear in mind that if an agent for some reason fails to pass on their deposit or the balance of their rental, they could lose their holiday.

Maid service is offered at many villas, the owners' or rental company's easiest way of knowing whether their clients are taking care of the property. In some cases the maid service is obligatory, and it almost always entails an extra cost to the visitors. Some grander properties also offer a cook, whose wages can be offset to some extent by the savings she will make in local purchases.

Most visitors to Tuscany arrive by air at **Pisa,** whose tower was accidentally immortalised by the blunders of architect Bonanno Pisano. His inadequate foundations have assured Pisa of a place on the principal tourist route, until, that is, the leaning tower finally falls. The tower (now closed), cathedral and baptistery are so inundated with visitors that nearby shops and restaurants are greatly overpriced. Self-catering in the centre of Pisa comes only at a premium, although some apartments on offer have an agreeable aspect over the River Arno.

Pisa lies within easy reach by motorway of the north Tuscan coast, although a spur of the same motorway separates some of the best beaches from the villas and apartments on offer. This certainly applies at **Forte dei Marmi**, reckoned by many to be the most chic of the Tuscan resorts. Concessionaires control the shore, keeping the yellow-grey sand clean and tidy . . . at a price. Restaurants here seem particularly expensive. The season is longer than elsewhere because of the number of second homes belonging to prosperous Italians, who fill the resort at weekends. The best villas stand among the pine trees behind the resort, but very few of these are available to rent.

Immediately south lies **Marina di Pietrasanta**, with beautiful long flat sands gently sloping into the sea, a friendly, rather unpretentious resort shared by middle-class Italians and a British self-catering enclave. Pietrasanta has fewer problems with the motorway and is ideal for families with young children that do not expect an over-vigorous nightlife. Next door, **Lido di Camaiore** is an undistinguished resort with a less attractive beach.

Viareggio, just to the south, is a package-tour paradise. Many of its apartments are run by the local hotels as a cheap alternative, though Viareggio itself is far from cheap. The beaches, mostly private, charge quite amazing sums for the use of a deckchair or a lilo. During the season visitors have to get up early to stake a claim to a strip of sand. Convenient for day-trips to Lucca or Pisa, Viareggio has a lively nightlife but is totally lacking in sophisticated entertainment.

Continuing south, **Livorno** (Leghorn), the second largest town in Tuscany, has a number of up-market flats and houses to rent along the Viale Italia, the wide sea-front road embellished with palm and pine trees. But the port and its beaches are severely polluted, and some parts of the town are seedy and dangerous after dark.

Below Livorno are several tiny, nondescript resorts, of which the best of a poor bunch is **Marina di Castagneto Donoratico**, at the end of a road that leads into the sea. Some of its apartments have thin walls and only rudimentary plumbing.

Once the coastline gives way to rocky headlands and coves, the villages take on a special charm. Just inland,

Campiglia Marittima has splendid views, thermal springs and five restaurants, including a bustling trattoria. One of the most attractive villages, **Populonia**, named after the Etruscan god of wine, stands high on a hill overlooking the sea and its ancient acropolis. Self-catering development here has so far been restrained and tasteful.

On the southern side of the promontory stands the fishing port of **Piombino**, with flats and rooms to rent along the quay. From here ferries go to the islands of the Tyrrhenian Sea, including the eight-mile voyage to **Elba**, temporary home of the exiled Emperor Napoleon. Elba, a thickly wooded and mountainous island, seems much more attractive after dark, when the day-trippers have departed. Its self-catering centre is **Porto Azzurro** on the eastern coast, whose harbour is full of expensive yachts during the summer. The open-air cafés shamelessly overcharge and the beach is cramped, but the port is hugely fashionable with many luxury villas to rent.

Virtually opposite Porto Azzurro on the mainland, the remote promontory of **Punta Ala** has a fine beach and a series of artificial villages with luxury villas and modern apartments; the most expensive form part of a yacht harbour where visitors without yachts seem decidedly unwelcome. The whole area is intensively geared to sports enthusiasts. There is no indigenous population, and, apart from a few bars, little to do at night.

The fortified town of **Castiglione della Pescaia**, to the south-east, is much more vivacious and has an old-world charm to go with its splendid sandy beach. The resort, once a quiet fishing village, now has an embryonic marina; it can be extremely crowded in midsummer. It is undergoing major new development, much of it self-catering.

Very few properties are available for rent along the undeveloped coastal strip running to the south. However, they return in abundance on the peninsula of **Monte Argentario**, a fashionable weekend watering-hole for affluent Romans. **Orbetello**, a tiny town on the narrow isthmus, has a number of apartments but no real beach. **Port'Ercole** on the southern side of the peninsula, is equally bereft of beaches but has a superbly picturesque harbour. There are houses to rent on the hillside above. **Porto Santo Stefano**, on the north-west corner, accommodates millionaires' yachts. Its restaurants are chic and expensive, like its shops, which offer the latest Rome and Paris fashions at Rome and Paris prices. From Porto Santo Stefano boats run to the island of **Giglio**, where the Etruscans are thought to have planted some of their first vines, carried from Asia Minor. Vineyards continue to flourish amid its rocky outcrop. The principal resort, **Campese**, has a shingle and sand beach, a few villas and beautiful clear water, ideal for scuba-diving.

Pisa is the airport for **Florence**, an hour's journey by train. The capital of Tuscany, Florence is a magnet for tourists, each anxious to capture a flavour of the Renaissance that made the city great. Medieval Florence had the moneybags of Europe and used its profits to pioneer not only Renaissance art but also economics, medicine, physics and philosophy, and to foster the creative genius of both Michelangelo and Leonardo da Vinci.

Some of the grand buildings belonging to the ruling family, the Medicis, now provide self-catering accommodation; but the period furnishings are far from ideal for children. Many apartments close to the centre are cramped and dark, a consequence of the austere architecture of the Renaissance. Unless your flat comes with a pass for the blue zone, parking may prove well-nigh impossible. Wrongly parked foreign cars will be towed away to a vehicle pound that may well be closer to Pisa than Florence. If you intend to devote your entire self-catering holiday to Florence, the best means of getting there is undoubtedly by train, the best means of getting around the city by bus. Florence is far from cheap, but its prices are not as outrageous as those at Venice or Rome.

Villas are available near two interesting towns between Pisa and Florence: Lucca and Pistoia. **Lucca**, north-east of Pisa, was once a self-contained city-state protected by its huge red ramparts. It remains pleasingly off the tourist track, a medieval microcosm of narrow streets and little houses. However, parking is difficult and there are remarkably few restaurants to cater for the local population, let alone for visitors. **Pistoia**, north-west of Florence, offers another excursion into the Middle Ages, with winding, narrow streets leading to a beautiful cathedral square.

In the broad strip of land that marks traditional Tuscany, running south and south-west of Florence to and even beyond Siena, there are many properties available in charming old towns and villages, notably **San Miniato**, with its fine Renaissance squares, **Vagliagli**, overlooking classic Chianti vineyards, and **Lucignano**, south of Siena, deep in beautiful wooded countryside. **Volterra**, west of Siena, has flats to rent within its medieval walls, and villas in the rugged surroundings. The town makes few concessions to tourism, and its restaurants are excellent value.

The same cannot be said of **San Gimignano**, whose fourteenth-century towers are irresistible to visitors: their sheer volume in summer makes restaurants impossibly crowded, and the food rushed and mediocre. The centre of the town is closed to traffic, a welcome relief unless you plan to use it as a food shopping centre.

Siena is just far enough away from Florence to deter the main bulk of summer coach-visitors, and a visit, however brief, will be richly rewarding, as it is second only to Florence as an artistic centre. Siena has preserved not only its medieval architecture but also its strong family rivalry – manifested each year in a furious and dangerous horse race around the magnificent central square, the Piazza del Campo. The prize is the *palio*, which gives its name to the race itself, a standard inscribed with the coat of arms of the city. Self-catering accommodation at the time of the *palio* (usually 2 July and 16 August) is at a premium, but during the rest of the year is widely available, though not always within the city walls. Parking within Siena is extremely arduous: leave the car on the outskirts.

In east and south-east Tuscany, fewer houses are available, except in the medieval walled village of **Monte San Savino** midway between Siena and Arezzo. It has 18 restored and comfortable apartments in separate houses offered for weekly lets and served (except on Mondays) by a jolly *osteria* offering particularly good-value wine from the local estate. Some flats are advertised in the larger towns of this area. There are mixed opinions about **Arezzo**, south-east of Florence. Its medieval centre of sloping meandering streets offers little accommodation; instead, most self-catering apartments are in the modern, disagreeable outskirts. **Cortona**, an ancient walled town to the south, seems a much less frenetic centre, and more likely to appeal to visitors eager to escape the crowds. **Montalcino**, due south of Siena, is a charming hill town and wine centre off the tourist routes with superb views of the surrounding plains. **Pienza**, beautifully preserved, has an absolute ban on wheeled traffic, which makes it exceptionally quiet – no doubt, for some, too quiet in the evenings. **Montepulciano**, a great Renaissance centre, has superb architecture but hazardously steep streets, making it unsuitable for the young, the infirm and the old.

Getting there

Galileo Galilei airport, one mile south-west of Pisa, 50 miles west of Florence, is the principal gateway to Tuscany. Direct flights (1½ hours) leave London from Heathrow or Gatwick throughout the year. Visitors to northern Tuscany may find Bologna (1½ hours) a useful alternative, especially in the peak season when Pisa is heavily in demand. Those staying on the Argentario peninsula can fly instead all the year round to Rome (2 hours) (see separate entry). During the summer many charter flights operate to each of these destinations from regional airports, including Birmingham, Belfast, Bristol, Glasgow and Manchester.

Motorail is available from Boulogne to Milan and, more conveniently, Bologna, during the summer. Overnight sleepers for travellers without cars are also available to Pisa: the journey from London takes about 24 hours.

By road, the route from Ostende via Cologne and Frankfurt takes advantage of toll-free motorways, crossing Switzerland to Milan, Florence and the Italian autostrada network. From Boulogne and Calais, a slightly shorter alternative is available via Luxemburg. If you fill up there with cheaper petrol, it may also cost virtually the same. The journey to Florence is about 900 miles, to Siena about 1000 miles, almost entirely by motorway, and could be achieved by indefatigable drivers in less than 24 hours.

Local transport

Tuscany has an extensive network of bus services, but there is little attempt at co-ordination between the various small companies. Where there should be a connection, one bus is often timed to leave a few minutes ahead of another due to arrive from a different direction. A single company may organise both a scheduled service and coach excursions, but the scheduled service is invariably much the cheaper.

Even if you have a car, rail travel between the larger cities such as Florence and Siena avoids parking problems. Away from the main routes, country services (*locale*) stop interminably at every station and are an extremely slow, if entertaining, means of transport. At larger stations expect a huge scrum at the ticket office in the few minutes before a train is due to depart.

Weather

Averages	Jan	Feb	Mar	Apr	May	Jun
Temperature	46	49	57	66	73	80
Sun hours	4	5	5	7	9	10
Rainy days	8	8	8	8	8	7
Sea temp.	47	46	47	53	61	69

Averages	Jul	Aug	Sep	Oct	Nov	Dec
Temperature	84	84	78	69	55	49
Sun hours	11	11	8	7	5	4
Rainy days	3	4	6	8	10	10
Sea temp.	75	74	71	63	57	52

Inland temperatures tend to be more extreme than on the coast, and cities can be stifling in midsummer. Tuscany remains agreeably warm and dry in autumn but can be disappointingly wet in spring.

Umbria

The land of the walnut and the black truffle, birthplace of St Francis and a host of other saints, scene of little battles and battlemented towers, Umbria is the very heart of Italy. South-east of Tuscany, entirely landlocked, its only water of consequence is the undistinguished Lake Trasimeno. The west consists of a patchwork plain of cultivated fields rising gently towards wooded hillside. The south is dominated by a bleak, inhospitable plateau. In the east the convulsions left by ancient volcanoes produce an eerie skyline blended with medieval towns taking advantage of the natural contours.

Umbria is less fashionable than Tuscany and less has been spent on restoring its rural villas and farmhouses, many of which still have antique wiring and spasmodic plumbing. The better houses belong to wealthy Romans who have little reason to rent them out, so the choice is more limited than it is in Tuscany, and the market is principally in the hands of recognised companies. However, for holiday-makers not requiring a private swimming-pool, Umbria has a great deal to offer, and is a rapidly expanding self-catering centre. Its principal disadvantage is that unlike Tuscany, which has both Florence and Siena, Umbria does not possess any single city to which it is worth devoting an entire holiday, and its main places of interest are widely dispersed. It is therefore difficult to select a single self-catering centre from which to explore.

The capital, **Perugia**, is famous for its university, and many collegiate buildings are rented out (both officially and unofficially) in the long summer vacation. It is important to find an apartment with a parking permit, for without one parking in the centre will be one long battle against the authorities. The principal and most elegant street, the Corso Vannucci, is closed to traffic, so accommodation here will not be noisy – but it will be expensive. Most of the interesting shops and buildings are

UMBRIA

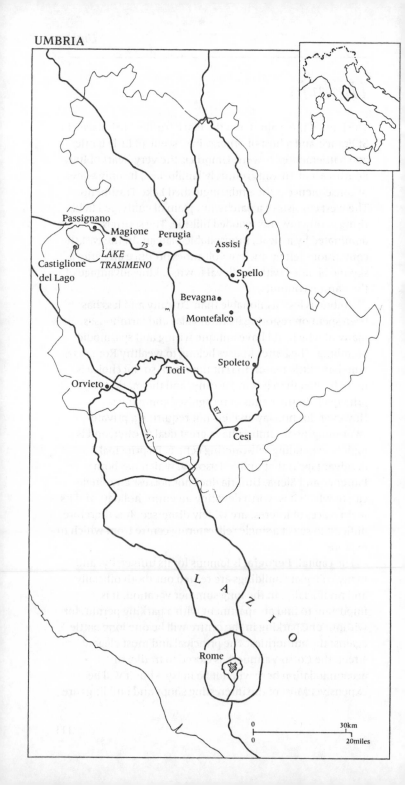

within easy walking distance, skirted by steep, dark alleyways.

To the north-west, Lake Trasimeno stands on the border between Umbria and Tuscany. It offers a full range of facilities, including swimming, sailing and windsurfing, but dismal scenery. The lake's resorts, **Castiglione del Lago**, **Passignano** and **Magione**, are equally uninspired, although Castiglione does have several lively restaurants.

Some way south, **Orvieto** has a few apartments among its narrow cobbled streets, close to the spectacular cathedral. The town, perched on a long-extinguished volcano, is noted for its exceptional local white wine.

South-east of Perugia, **Assisi**, the burial-place of St Francis, the patron saint of Italy, has a number of villas for rent nearby but little self-catering accommodation in the town. This is a pity, because Assisi takes on a much more attractive air after the tourist buses have left and the pilgrims are back in their hotels. Apart from its commercialism, Assisi has remained virtually unchanged since the Middle Ages, honeycombed with narrow, sloping streets, clattering cobbles and balconied squares.

Striking south-east, rather more austere farmhouse accommodation is available near **Bevagna**, an agreeable little country town in a rich valley, and **Spello**, a hill town with Roman fortifications and winding medieval streets. Further south, **Montefalco** has apartments near the central piazza with superb views.

South-west of Montefalco and south of Perugia, three more medieval hillside towns have a number of villas nearby. **Todi**, closer to Perugia, stands in Gothic splendour, grim and forbidding after dark. **Spoleto**, overlooking delightful wooded countryside, has very few tourists. Eating dinner *al fresco* is particularly attractive in the medieval centre, where the narrow streets are lit by ancient lanterns. However, much of the accommodation is located in the dull, modern town below, and during June and July an arts festival ensures that it is in very short supply. **Cesi**, at the foot of a mountain, was a medieval bastion of the Pope; the ancient walls still survive.

ITALY

Getting there

Rome (see page 115), 2 hours from London, is by far the most convenient arrival point by air. As a hire car is almost always necessary in Umbria, it is also possible to fly to Pisa or Bologna (see page 109), both 1½ hours from London, and drive from there.

The weekly Motorail service from Boulogne to Bologna (see page 109) makes the journey far less arduous. For holiday-makers without cars, Perugia and Orvieto can also be reached by rail, usually only by changing at Milan.

The journey by car passes through Tuscany (see page 109) and takes at least 24 hours. Perugia and Orvieto are both on motorway routes south of Florence.

Local transport

Umbria has very limited links by bus, and a car is essential for most holiday-makers staying in a villa. Visits to major cities such as Rome, Florence, Siena, Perugia or Orvieto may be more convenient by rail. Domestic Italian rail services are fast, reliable and extremely good value.

Weather

Averages	Jan	Feb	Mar	Apr	May	Jun
Temperature	47	50	58	67	74	81
Sun hours	4	5	5	7	9	11
Rainy days	8	8	8	8	8	6

Averages	Jul	Aug	Sep	Oct	Nov	Dec
Temperature	85	85	79	70	56	50
Sun hours	11	12	8	7	5	4
Rainy days	3	3	6	8	10	10

The north of Umbria is warm and dry in autumn but can be wet in spring. In the south, temperatures in midsummer can be particularly severe.

Rome

Expect almost all self-catering accommodation in Rome to be cramped and slightly shabby. There is a great shortage of flats in the city and therefore very little appears on the tourist market, as the Italian owners can obtain long lets among their fellow citizens at high prices. Making contact with an academic institution may provide a promising lead, as students and teaching staff tend to leave the city during the long, hot summer vacation.

It is important to establish the exact location of your prospective apartment, because many districts of the city are a long way from the principal sights. The most attractive area in which to stay is close to the centre of what was Ancient Rome, on either side of the Via del Corso. However, you need a permit to park your car here, and vehicles infringing the regulations are frequently towed away. Even those legitimately parked all too often are vandalised, with the radio always a tempting target.

Getting there

From London and Manchester (2½ hours) by daily scheduled flights to Leonardo da Vinci airport (commonly called Fiumicino), 18 miles south-west of the city. The airport has separate but adjacent terminals for international and domestic flights. Charter flights operate from several regional UK airports to Ciampino airport, 8 miles south-east of the centre. Strikes at Rome's airports by air traffic controllers or baggage handlers are regular phenomena, especially at peak holiday periods.

By Motorail, from Boulogne to Bologna (see page 109) and then by car on the motorway. For travellers without cars, there's a direct overnight train service from London (24 hours).

The entire journey by car passes through Tuscany (see page 109) and involves an overnight stop for all but the most determined driver.

Local transport

Rome has an efficient and frequent bus service. A bus route map is available at most tourist offices and news-stands, and tickets are on sale at news-stands and bars. There is a uniform fare throughout the city. Weekly and monthly passes are also available. Passengers are required to enter buses by the rear door and leave by the front or the centre.

Two partially underground 'metro' services operate in the city. One runs from the main railway station, Termini, to the Colisseum and on to Ostia Antica, the seaport of Ancient Rome. Most of the other tourist sights have convenient stops on the second metro line, which runs north-west from Via Anagnina to Ottaviano near the Vatican City.

All public transport becomes very infrequent between 1 and 4 p.m., the Roman siesta, when traffic throughout the city is agreeably light.

Weather

Averages	Jan	Feb	Mar	Apr	May	Jun
Temperature	51	55	59	66	73	82
Sun hours	4	5	6	7	8	9
Rainy days	6	6	7	9	8	8

Averages	Jul	Aug	Sep	Oct	Nov	Dec
Temperature	86	86	79	72	61	55
Sun hours	11	10	8	6	4	4
Rainy days	7	7	5	7	9	8

Rome in midsummer can be oppressively hot. In winter, even as late as March, plan for sub-zero temperatures at night, and occasional snow. The best weather conditions are in late spring or early autumn.

Adriatic Riviera

Apart from a few grand, *fin-de-siècle* hotels, the Adriatic
Riviera has never encouraged tourists who regard the
hotel grounds as the outer limits of their holiday. The
management of all but the most luxurious establishments
prefers guests to leave the place deserted in favour of the
beach, a bar or a nightclub; he provides meals but little else
in the way of amenities or entertainment. Those who opt
in favour of self-catering on the Adriatic will be therefore
very little disadvantaged.

Unfortunately, the great asset of the Adriatic Riviera –
superb sandy beaches – has been damaged by increasing
pollution. No doubt it was always present: but in recent
years it has become so severe that in some parts the colour
of the sea has turned from azure to yellow-brown. The
local authorities are making strenuous efforts to remove
the outward signs of pollution, but the pollution has done
severe damage to the popularity and credibility of the
Adriatic as a tourist destination.

The Riviera begins in the north at **Grado,** an island
connected to the mainland by a causeway. Its architecture
is a mixture of medieval and imperial Austrian style, for
Grado was once part of the Austro-Hungarian Empire and
still receives a large number of Austrian and German
tourists. Some large older properties have been divided
into holiday apartments, but most are some way from the
agreeable sandy beach.

The self-catering centre lies to the west beyond the
Marana Lagoon at **Lignano Sabbiadoro,** a flat, slightly
marshy peninsula rapidly reaching saturation point in new
development. Lignano has apartments and some
semblance of nightlife; Sabbiadoro is rather more up-
market, with luxury villas on offer among the pine trees.

The coastline continues south-west to **Caorle,** an
obscure fishing village with camping, some small hotels,
but otherwise only simple rooms to let. Just outside,
however, there are plans for a new self-catering
development, including a substantial swimming-pool.

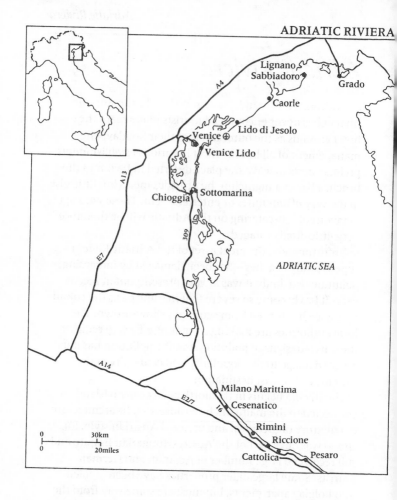

Further south-west, the coast is dominated by the huge resort of **Lido di Jesolo,** a child of the 1960s package-tour industry boom, created out of nothing. It resembles in many ways a film set, stretching back barely three streets from the shore. The beach is truly magnificent: ten miles of golden sand and, unlike most of the rest of Italy, with no charge for admission.

However, Lido di Jesolo is not uniformly attractive. The south is a little seedy, full of cheap hotels and restaurants, and a few apartment blocks that have seen better days. The centre is dominated by large hotels, some with swimming-pools, which are open to non-residents – an added bonus if your self-catering accommodation, mainly smart apartments, happens to be close by. In the north, where the beach becomes so wide that from the rear it is difficult to make out the shoreline, self-catering villages sit like lonely little oases, a long way from most of the amenities. Lido di Jesolo is 11 miles from Venice, a good hour's drive along a busy road, and should not be confused with the genuine **Venice Lido,** an island directly opposite the city with fashionable and expensive beaches. It is possible to take your car to the centre of the Lido by ferry, avoiding most of the hassle of unloading luggage; and Venice is only ten or fifteen minutes away. Self-catering accommodation, both villas and flats, is available but difficult to book from the UK.

In **Venice** itself, a number of apartments are on offer, many owned by affluent Italians taking their summer holidays elsewhere. Some have rather grand furnishings a little vulnerable to children; nearly all are cramped and without air-conditioning, a problem during the high-season heat. If you do book an apartment in Venice, find out before you travel exactly where it is in relation to the main water-bus routes; and remember that you may have to carry your luggage some distance. **Chioggia,** at the southern point of the Venetian lagoon, is a charming old town but with very little in the way of self-catering accommodation. The principal place nearby to find both villas and apartments is **Sottomarina,** an entirely artificial resort built among pine trees. Its beach is particularly safe for children.

Further south, **Milano Marittima,** literally 'Milan-by-the-Sea', consists almost entirely of private villas in secluded grounds. They are used almost exclusively by affluent Italian families, though occasionally advertised to let in the leading Milan and Turin newspapers, *Corriere della Sera* and *La Stampa*.

The Adriatic coast now gives way to a series of package-tour resorts, whose beaches charge for admission but which are ideal for children and watersports enthusiasts.

Unlike in France, however, very few have restaurants able to offer more than simple snacks – reflecting the fact that most visitors go back to their hotels to eat. **Cesenatico,** the most northerly resort, has the fewest UK visitors; its canal port is charming, with quayside bars and plenty of evening entertainment. **Rimini,** the most famous, has more than 30 nightclubs spearheading a frenetic nightlife that goes on almost to dawn; this can be a huge disadvantage if your apartment happens to be close to the sea-front, as many are. A dangerous and busy main road separates almost all the self-catering accommodation from the shore, which is mile upon mile of pale sands. In pre-pollution days, the beach was always packed with end-to-end parosols; it remains to be seen whether Rimini makes a successful comeback.

South of Rimini, **Riccione,** a more sophisticated resort with a good shopping centre, nevertheless has the common disadvantage of a main road akin to a Grand Prix circuit that separates most of the self-catering accommodation from the beach. Only in the north of the resort does the main road swing inland, and this area is dominated by the best hotels.

Cattolica closes its main streets to traffic after dark. The area behind the sea-front, where many apartments are located, is, however, particularly noisy at night, with several lively discos. Cattolica is extremely popular with young holiday-makers.

Pesaro, the most southerly of the Adriatic resorts, has plenty of accommodation that opens directly on to the wide sand. Some apartments in the old quarter receive very little direct sunlight.

Getting there
Venice and the northern Adriatic By air, from Stansted (2 hours); Gatwick, Heathrow (2¼ hours); Bristol, Cardiff, Manchester (2½ hours); Glasgow (3 hours). Marco Polo airport is eight miles north of Venice.

By rail, if you can afford it, on the Orient Express, or by less romantic trains to Venice; the journey from London takes about 27 hours.

By Motorail from Boulogne to Bologna (see page 109). Note that cars are not permitted in Venice (which has entirely water-borne transport) and must be parked on the outskirts of the city.

Rimini and the southern Adriatic By air, from Bristol, Birmingham, East Midlands, Gatwick, Luton (2½ hours); Manchester (3 hours); Glasgow (3¼ hours).

By Motorail, overnight from Paris to Rimini.

By road, follow the route to Tuscany as far as Milan (see page 109), then strike west.

Local transport

Venice and the northern Adriatic The water-bus is the cheapest and most efficient way of travelling around Venice and many neighbouring ports and islands. A gondola ride is essential for travellers visiting Venice for the first time. Make this a shared experience with another family or new-found friends, as a gondola will take four adults and half a dozen children quite comfortably. Avoid picking up your gondola in the lagoon, as the water can be quite choppy.

Rimini and the southern Adriatic A trolley-bus service operates every few minutes during the summer between Rimini and Riccione. Elsewhere, buses are cheap but crowded; tickets can be bought in advance from local shops and from most bars and even restaurants.

Weather
Venice and the northern Adriatic

Averages	Jan	Feb	Mar	Apr	May	Jun
Temperature	43	46	54	63	70	77
Sun hours	3	4	4	6	8	9
Rainy days	6	6	7	9	8	8
Sea temp.	46	45	46	52	60	68

Averages	Jul	Aug	Sep	Oct	Nov	Dec
Temperature	81	81	75	66	52	46
Sun hours	10	10	7	6	4	3
Rainy days	7	7	5	7	9	8
Sea temp.	74	73	70	62	56	51

Apart from at the peak of the season, the weather can be cloudy on this part of the Adriatic coast. The sunniest months are

121

July and August, when the high temperatures make Venice an arduous and often odorous destination.

Rimini and the southern Adriatic

Averages	Jan	Feb	Mar	Apr	May	Jun
Temperature	52	55	59	66	73	82
Sun hours	3	4	4	5	8	9
Rainy days	8	5	8	8	7	7
Sea temp.	52	48	50	55	63	70

Averages	Jul	Aug	Sep	Oct	Nov	Dec
Temperature	86	86	79	70	61	55
Sun hours	10	8	6	4	2	3
Rainy days	4	5	6	8	11	9
Sea temp.	73	75	73	66	61	55

Although temperatures remain relatively high, this part of the Adriatic has only spasmodic sunshine outside the summer period. The sunniest months are July and August.

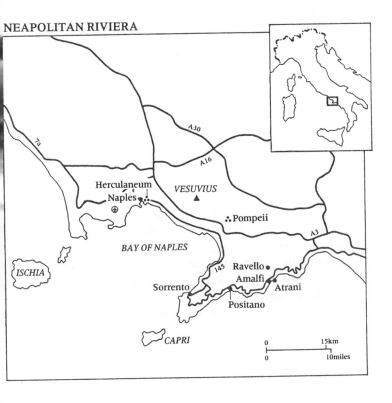

Neapolitan Riviera

The Neapolitan Riviera has a mixture of villas and apartments on offer, but it is not an area for a beach holiday, as much of the coast consists of rocks running sheer into the sea. Even the best beaches are little more than strips of grey, lava-based sand, the consequence of the eruptions of Vesuvius across the centuries. Its true attraction is the scenery: stunning views of Vesuvius and the Bay of Naples; the islands of Ischia and Capri; and history in suspended animation at Pompeii and Herculaneum.

Sorrento's apartments are all on top of the peninsula that completes the southern curve of the Bay of Naples and are some way from the 'beaches' below, to which access is

123

possible only by way of lifts. Swimming is dangerous because of underwater rocks, some beaches have occasional deposits of tar, and all are spoilt by the presence of seaweed. The major hotels have tried to overcome these problems by constructing pontoons next to the shore, but non-residents are not welcome in high season. Those who rent apartments in the town centre may find the noise level conspicuous, both from discos and from hooting cars in the early evening traffic. Many restaurants cater especially for the lower end of the package-tour market, offering bacon, egg, and sausage instead of tagliatelle.

Amalfi has some fine houses for rent in the narrow streets of the town, a masterpiece of pre-Renaissance Italy. Their secluded courtyards provide essential shade against the summer sun. The beach, however, is too small to cope with the influx of day-trippers. Evenings here can be dull.

High above Amalfi, behind the vineyards and lemon groves, the once-independent republic of **Ravello** offers a secluded charm and a truly breathtaking view of the sea and coast below. Its best villas share a communal swimming-pool and are splendidly well equipped, with central heating for the colder winter months.

Within easy walking distance of Amalfi, the forgotten fishing village of **Atrani** has apartments in an ancient mansion complete with swimming-pool. Atrani's restaurants are outstanding, and, as there is no hotel, visitors are few and far between.

Positano's location is so superb that its practical difficulties may be overlooked . . . for a while. Almost all its self-catering apartments are high on the hillside, a long and arduous climb from the two tiny beaches (one a short walk from the centre). A shuttle bus runs up and down in summer, but long queues are common.

Many apartments in Naples may seem cheap, but they are frequently cramped and stifling during summer. The standard of hygiene in Naples restaurants can be unsatisfactory, and eating in the poorer parts of the city is not recommended.

Getting there

By air to Naples from Birmingham, Luton, Gatwick (2¾ hours); Manchester (3 hours); Glasgow (3¼ hours). Capodochino airport is four miles north of Naples.

For details of Motorail, see Tuscany (page 109).

Local transport

Driving a car in or near Naples can be a hazardous experience: the local Neapolitans drive at sustained high speed even in narrow streets, and the coast road to Sorrento consists of endless bends above a cliff edge.

An excellent railway, the Circumvesuviana operates from Naples to Sorrento by way of the famous ruins at Herculaneum and Pompeii. Local buses are fast, numerous and reliable. A hydrofoil also links Naples and Sorrento. Many taxis in the Neapolitan area have disconnected their meters, so negotiate the fare before hand.

Weather

Averages	Jan	Feb	Mar	Apr	May	Jun
Temperature	57	59	63	66	70	77
Sun hours	4	4	6	7	9	9
Rainy days	8	7	7	5	4	1
Sea temp.	58	58	59	60	64	70

Averages	Jul	Aug	Sep	Oct	Nov	Dec
Temperature	83	82	78	72	63	61
Sun hours	11	9	8	6	4	3
Rainy days	0	1	3	6	9	9
Sea temp.	73	75	71	66	63	58

The Neapolitan Riviera has mild but rather wet winters; summer temperatures are extremely hot inland but more moderate near the sea.

Portugal

For the British, the southernmost province of Portugal, the Algarve, is a home from home. Around 8000 expatriates live there permanently, many of them renting out their houses in high season to supplement their pensions. British tourists travel there in their tens of thousands, more than from any other country, attracted by the mild winters, prolonged summers and outstanding beaches. The Portuguese, ever eager to please, have done their best to turn the Algarve into a little England. Pubs with British beer, self-service hamburger restaurants, British tinned food in the supermarkets, and estate agents with a hyperbole in every sentence, together tend to make parts of the Algarve disquietingly like an English south-coast seaside resort; all that is missing is the pier.

The boom in tourism continues unchecked, and with it the construction of new villas and apartments. This building work may not be quite on the grand scale of the 1980s, when land and labour were both cheap, but it is still a source of noise in all the major resorts from very early in the morning. Although Portugal has succeeded in preventing, with one or two exceptions, the high-rise concrete jungle of the Spanish Costas from happening on the Algarve, smaller blocks have simply spread outwards to swamp existing settlements. In some areas new holiday villages have sprung up with admirable facilities but totally devoid of any authentic character.

Portugal's coast borders the Atlantic Ocean, making the

water cooler and much rougher than the Mediterranean – especially on the windy west coast. The movement of the sea is also a contributory factor in reducing pollution, and Portugal's beaches are among the cleanest in Europe. Only Estoril and Cascais, near the sea lanes into Lisbon, have serious pollution problems.

Portugal offers a great deal of accommodation that falls between the traditional categories of a hotel and self-catering. Many hotels have bought adjacent apartments where holiday-makers are encouraged, even expected, to eat regularly in the hotel restaurant. Behind the coastal areas, a number of Portuguese manors – once owned by the great aristocrats – have apartments or cottages in the grounds, offering visitors the option of taking meals in the main house; breakfast is often included in the rental price. Holiday villages usually have a complex that includes a restaurant, enabling some of their clientele to opt for a half-board arrangement. In each of these categories, the kitchens in the apartments may be extremely small or poorly equipped, an incentive for holiday-makers to eat in the restaurant. The central complex may have ambitious facilities, including more than one swimming-pool, a full range of shops, discos and a gymnasium. These huge, dedicated developments are very much a Portuguese speciality.

Most villas in a self-catering village and many apartments include maid service in the price. However, the average Portuguese maid has a very firm idea of what she is required to do within the terms of her contract. She will make the beds, change the linen (nearly always provided in Portugal) once a week, sweep up and whisk a duster around the rooms. She may well come in six days a week, but never on Sundays. She will not normally, even if you offer to pay her a great many escudos, wash up. As virtually none of the apartments and very few villas on offer in Portugal possess a dishwasher, this can be an inconvenience. But it may be possible to arrange through your tour operator or rental company for the maid to wash up.

Water heaters in most apartments and some villas

operate on gas, with a central supply in large towns, individual gas containers in rural areas. In the early 1980s five British tourists in rented apartments with gas heaters died of carbon monoxide poisoning, due to unsatisfactory ventilation and faulty installation. The Portuguese authorities responded with a rigorous inspection programme of all gas heaters in registered self-catering accommodation, requiring each apartment block or house to display a safety certificate. But many unregistered properties, usually those let through direct advertising, have not been inspected. Any risk can be sharply reduced by leaving the windows open at night.

Solar heating has replaced gas in some areas, particularly for hot water. On cloudy days this may mean that the water never reaches more than a lukewarm temperature, and even after prolonged sunshine it rarely stays hot until the following morning. Plan for an afternoon bath, or stay in a property with standard heating arrangements. Interruptions to both the electricity and water supply are common, especially during the peak tourist season, albeit for only a few hours at a time.

In price terms, Portugal is something of a paradox. Although costs are rising, in comparative terms, the prices of restaurant meals, bar drinks and incidentals such as sweets and ice-cream are among the lowest of all European resort areas. On the other hand, inclusive packages – of villa or apartment plus flight – are among the most expensive. This is mainly because there are very few charter flights to Lisbon, and the demand for flights to Faro in the Algarve far exceeds the supply in high season. Unlike getting to France, Italy or Spain, there is no credible Motorail or rail alternative, and driving the whole way from the UK is arduous and time-consuming.

What to take with you

As you will almost certainly travel to Portugal by air, both luggage space and weight will be at a premium. But still pack towels that can double up for bath and beach, as in all but the most luxurious villas Portuguese bath-towels are too small. Against that, self-catering accommodation in Portugal is more likely to provide a kettle and a teapot than in almost any other European country, as tea is drunk regularly by the Portuguese.

Nevertheless, tea is slightly more expensive, as are instant coffee and vacuum-packed mature cheese and high-quality bacon. Other food-related items worth taking from the UK include plastic rubbish bags, kitchen foil and cling-wrap. You can expect to find far more British fads and fancies in the shops than you can in other European countries, a result of the number of British expatriates in Portugal.

Villas and apartments vary considerably in the quality of their kitchens, and it may be best to assume the worst, particularly if you are staying in a rural area. Accordingly, take a tin-opener, corkscrew and a box of matches, together with some plastic egg-cups, a sharp kitchen knife, a pair of pliers, a set of small screwdrivers and a torch with new batteries. Also worth taking are an adaptor or some standard Continental two-pin plugs for use with a hair-drier or electric razor. Portugal has the uniform UK 220-volt AC supply.

Eating in

Portugal is quickly catching up with the concept of high-volume, high-turnover supermarkets, although there are very few of the size and scale of the hypermarkets prevalent in France. Large supermarkets exist only in cities, and a so-called supermarket (*supermercado*) in coastal tourist areas may well be the equivalent of a modest self-service shop in the UK. Some of them nevertheless persist in providing large trolleys quite unsuitable for the width of their aisles. The trolleys have often been purchased second-hand and the wheels should be checked if you are to avoid spilling the contents between the checkout and your hired car. Unfortunately, the distribution of goods in Portugal is on an equally small scale. In summer it is not uncommon for even quite large supermarkets to run out of some vital commodity, such as butter or salt. For this reason self-catering visitors are advised on arrival to make a comprehensive list of basic foodstuffs they may require for the entire holiday, and to make a visit to a supermarket their priority.

The Portuguese still like to patronise their local grocer (*mercearia*) or one of the multitude of family-run corner shops (*lugas*), which are unlikely to operate on a self-service principle. Expect them to stock many of the items available in a UK delicatessen, plus fresh fruit and vegetables, wine, bread, pasteurised milk and cheese. The prices may be higher, but they are more likely to stock up-market British brand-names than are supermarkets.

A specialist dairy (*laticinios*) is comparatively rare, but may stock better-quality produce. Eggs (*ovos*) are sold in four grades, A to D; D is the best but not necessarily the largest. Butter (*manteiga*) is available unsalted, semi-salted and salted. British visitors may find Portuguese salted butter very much an acquired taste.

The greengrocer (*lugar da hortaliças*) has been superseded by the open market (*mercado*), which operates two or three days a week in most towns and villages (although a few specialist shops sell sub-tropical fruit and vegetables from Madeira and the Azores). Portugal itself has an abundance of fresh vegetables, fruit and flowers. The most commonplace vegetable is the Portuguese cabbage (*couve portuguesa*), which is darker and larger than its British equivalent. Sometimes its leaves are sold shredded by the kilogramme, for use (with chicken stock, olive oil, sausage and potatoes) in the Portuguese national soup, *caldo verde*.

The market will also usually have a stall selling meat, although all towns and most villages will also possess a butcher's shop (*talho*). As in many Mediterranean countries, very little meat may be on display as it will generally be refrigerated; you may find that you may have to buy without seeing the produce. As cuts are not the same as they are in the UK, it is important to ask to see the meat and then to show the piece you require, especially as the mainstay of Portuguese meat, beef, can be disappointing. Although by crossbreeding local and imported stock, Portugal has improved dramatically the quality of its beef, it is still likely to be much tougher than beef sold in the UK. Ask for sirloin (*rosbife*) or fillet steak (*filé* or *lombo*), and beware of being palmed off with tougher meat that actually comes from a cow (*vaca*).

There is much less risk of lamb (*borrego*) being dressed up as mutton (*carneiro*) as most sheep are reared for their wool. The best buys are lamb chops (*vão de costeletas*) or saddle of lamb (*sela*); again, because the cuts are different, note that what you should be getting is a cut across the back of the animal providing a double chop or roast. Veal (*vitela*) is usually tender but quite expensive. Goat is an unfamiliar meat for most visitors, but, provided that it really is kid (*cabrito*), it can be tender and tasty. You may be offered the entire carcass for roasting – much too large for an average family on a self-catering holiday, unlesss you are sharing with friends or have a very large freezer. Offal (*ferssura*) may sound an unappetising prospect, but liver (*figado*) can be a good buy. In Lisbon, thinly sliced cooked liver (known as *iscas*), marinated in white wine and fried with ham, is a local delicacy.

Game is plentiful in Portugal, particularly rabbit (*coelho*) in the Algarve, where some of the cheaper hotels have been known to serve it, cooked in different ways, for an entire fortnight. In the Lisbon area, partridge (*perdiz*) is cheap and plentiful. Turkey (*peru*) is often sold in square chunks ready for a stew.

Chicken (*frango*) may also be sold in pieces. If you buy it at a market stall in the Algarve, you risk finding that the bird was reared on fish meal and that the taste has permeated the meat. Ready-prepared birds are usually available only in supermarkets.

Good pork (*porco*) seems to be on the decline and generally is more fatty than its British equivalent. It may be sold fresh by traditional butchers but otherwise more likely at the *charcutaria*, together with bacon, ham and sausages. Bacon is the same word in Portuguese, but to buy the nearest equilavent to British bacon, ask for *entremado* or *toucinho*, a cut from the fat belly of the pig. The *charcutaria* also sells pâtés, a number of pre-cooked dishes and cheese (*queijo*), which if imported remains something of a luxury item in Portugal. Local cheeses are named after the region in which they are made, and some have a quite extraordinary taste. The conservative British shopper will be safe enough if he or she asks for *queijo do Alentejo*, a hard mature ewe's-milk cheese or *queijo Castelâo*, indistinguishable from Dutch Edam.

As might be expected in a country with such a long seaboard, Portugal is renowned for its abundance of fresh fish and shellfish. Wherever you stay, fresh fish will be available, because even the most remote inland areas are still less then 150 miles from the Atlantic. Despite the influx of tourists, fishing remains one of Portugal's key industries. Much of the produce is sold in markets, or even on the beach. You can buy direct from a fisherman after breakfast or early evening, as fishing fleets often make two trips a day, avoiding the hottest hours. The most common fish are sardines (*sardinhas*) – not the little tiddlers found in tins in the UK, but a substantial meal, often available barbecued at the roadside or on the beach. Larger towns may still have a fishmonger (*peixaria*), where you are likely to find lobster (*lagosta*), prawns (*gambas*) and a fish similar to sole, called *linguado*. All these are expensive; better value are sea-bass (*robalo*) and hake (*pescada*), sometimes sold filleted or in cutlets.

The bakery (*padaria*) provides a variety of bread, depending on the region. You cannot go far wrong if you ask for home-baked bread, (*pão caseiro*). The baker's may well also be a pastry shop (*pastelaria*), offering a huge variety of pastries, cakes and biscuits beloved of the Portuguese. From about four o'clock onwards, the shop may be packed with people at little tables, eating cakes and drinking tea, a social custom started by the British in the last century.

The British also stimulated the production of port, largely to replace French claret, which became difficult to obtain during the Napoleonic, and indeed earlier, wars with France. The vines were planted on hitherto unproductive hillsides by the original estate owners, such as Croft and Sandeman, who were British entrepreneurs.

Port is still almost entirely exported, mainly to the UK, and, perhaps a little ironically, to France as well. In consequence, port is not particularly cheap in Portugal, even in supermarkets, while vintage port is difficult to obtain and extremely expensive.

Mateus Rosé is also largely exported; you may find the version for local consumption rather drier and probably no cheaper. Much better value is *vinho verde*, the so-called 'green wine', Portugal's real speciality. *Vinho verde* does not normally come in green bottles, nor is it green (the white variety is actually pale yellow) except in the sense of 'green' youth, lacking maturity. *Vinho verde* can be white or red; the white is more popular, and the red, though cheaper, may be too sharp for some British tastes.

Eating out

Restaurants in Portugal are among the cheapest in Europe, with fine cuisine and generous portions. Most of their owners make ends meet by cheap labour (the family), a limited number of dishes and indifferent décor. The restaurant run by a local pension (*pensão*) may be the best value in the smarter resort areas. Otherwise look for a tavern (*tasca*), distinguished by its stand-up bar for snacks and drinks. Beer-houses (*cervejarias*) often provide not only snacks but astonishing full meals. If you like fish, try one of the specialist seafood bars (*marisquerias*).

Unlike the Spanish, the Portuguese have similar meal-times to the British. Lunch is from around 12.30 to 2.30, dinner from about 8 to 9.30, earlier in rural areas. Only on national holidays is it traditional to eat very late – from about 10 to midnight. Many restaurants close on Mondays, especially in Lisbon and other large cities.

Irrespective of price, almost all Portuguese restaurants offer their clientele a range of savouries to eat while choosing their main meal. These may include small pieces of cheese, pâté and smoked ham, complete with toast and savoury butter, and dishes of olives, which are replenished throughout the meal. It is all too easy to ruin one's appetite long before the main course arrives. In more simple restaurants you will eat off a paper tablecloth, renewed for each customer, and be served your food in large earthenware pots, with the local wine in an earthenware jar.

The coffee at the end of a meal is something of a Portuguese ritual. Although now largely imported from Brazil instead of from Angola (and therefore less bitter), it will be offered in a small cup and will be strong unless you are careful to explain what you want. Espresso is the same as elsewhere, strong and in a medium-sized cup; *bica* is black and strong in a small cup; *garato* is served in a cup and is strong but with hot milk added; *carioca* is black but less strong and comes in a larger cup; *galao* is white, strong and served in a tall glass; *pingado* is a weaker version. To order coffee with milk, ask for *café com leite*.

Children

The Portuguese are closer to the British in their attitude to children, believing that there is a time and a place for them; but children are welcome in all but the most up-market restaurants in Lisbon and other large cities. As a rule, restaurants actually quote half-portions (*meias doses*) on the menu and are quite happy to provide them – to adults as well. The only food favoured by small children not readily available is yoghurt, although this is now stocked by larger supermarkers in packets complete with a tiny plastic spoon. Baby food is most easily purchased at a chemist's shop (*farmacia*).

Transport

The majority of self-catering holiday-makers arriving at Faro hire a car, which is essential for those staying anywhere outside the principal resorts. Car hire is relatively inexpensive, especially if arranged as part of a package deal when booking your accommodation. However, many of the rental vehicles are not in good condition; check the steering, brakes and the tyres, including the spare, before setting off. Be warned that

Portuguese drivers take huge risks, and many pay the penalty; one recent survey placed Portugal fourth highest in the world, behind only Kuwait, Mexico and Venezuela, in the accident stakes. Moreover, in rural districts the roads are badly maintained.

In the Lisbon area taxis are common; they are obliged by law to carry a list of fares in English, and by asking for it you may reduce the charge.

A railway runs along the coast between Lisbon and Cascais. There are overnight sleepers from Lisbon to the Algarve; the Algarve line runs from Lagos in the west as far as the Spanish border; but it is of little scenic interest. Allow plenty of time for buying tickets; the booking office is always chaotic. Express coaches connect Lisbon to the major resorts of the Algarve, where local buses are cheap and reliable.

Avoiding problems

Medical insurance is almost essential in Portugal to ensure priority treatment. For minor ailments, go to the chemist, who has considerable medical training and can dispense many quite powerful drugs available in the UK only on a doctor's prescription. In an emergency, dial 115 for the national ambulance service.

Portugal has few serious crime problems that might affect the holiday-maker, although petty theft is common in the major resorts. In Lisbon it is not advisable for women to travel alone on the public transport system at night.

Opening hours

On weekdays most shops open at 9.30 a.m., close for lunch at 1 p.m., re-open at 3 and close again at 7 p.m. In summer the lunch break may be longer, until 3.30 or 4, and closing time 7.30 or 8. Saturday is a half-day. The baker's, butcher's and fishmonger's open at around 7 a.m. and usually close for the day at 1 p.m. The baker's shop is open on Sunday morning in rural areas. The butcher's shop is closed all day on Sunday and Monday. Pastry shops and supermarkets open at about 9 a.m. and close at about 9 p.m., sometimes later. Markets tend to start at 7 a.m. and close by 1 p.m.

Most banks are open from 8.30 to 11.45 a.m. and from 1 p.m. to 2.45, Monday to Friday only: in Lisbon some branches may also re-open during the evenings from 6 to 9 p.m. Monday to Saturday. Many exchange bureaux also remain open at weekends in tourist areas.

Public holidays

1 January (New Year's Day); **Shrove Tuesday** (in February, varies from year to year); **Good Friday** and **Easter Sunday;** **25 April** (commemorating the 1974 Portuguese Revolution); **1 May** (Labour Day); **10 June** (Camões Day, in honour of the famous Portuguese poet); **Corpus Christi** (usually early June); **15 August** (the Feast of the Assumption of the Virgin Mary); **5 October** (Republic Day); **1 November** (All Saints' Day); **1 December** (Independence Day); **8 December** (the Feast of the Immaculate Conception); **25 December** (Christmas Day); Lisbon has an additional local holiday on **13 June.**

What to bring back

Hand-made jewellery in gold or silver
Embroidery
Tapestry
Hand-painted tiles
Ceramics
Copper
Leather bags, belts and shoes.

Tour operators

For details see page 213

Aer Lingus Holidays
Airlink Holidays
Airtours
Algarve Asset Management
Algarve Select
Allegro Holidays
Beach Villas
Bingley & Miller
Bowhill Holidays
Bridgeway Travel Services
Burstin Travel
Continental Villas
Cornisa Travel and Villas

Cosmos
Crockford Enterprises
CV Travel
ESP Travel and Leisure Services
European Villas
Exclusive Villas
Falcon de-Luxe Resorts
Fidesca Lda
Global Air Holidays
Grainger Properties
Hartland Holidays
Horizon Holidays
Lanterna Villas
Maclaine Holidays
Martyn Holidays
Memories Travel
Meon Travel
NAT Holidays
OSL
The Owners' Syndicate
Palm Luxury Villas
Palmer & Parker Holidays
Paloma Holidays
Patricia Wildblood
Portugal Connections

The Portuguese Property
  Bureau
Purely Portugal
Redwing Holidays
Rentavilla
Saga Holidays
Seasun Tentrek
Select Holidays
Something Special Travel
Starvillas
Thomson Holidays
Tjaerborg

The Travel Club
Travel Plus Holidays
The Villa Agency
Villa and Farm Holidays
The Villa Bureau
The Villa Holiday Centre
Villa Plus
Villa Select
VillaSeekers
Villashare
Villasun Holidays

The Algarve

The Algarve, once too distant from Britain to be a popular resort area, was transformed in the 1960s by the arrival of the air package-tour business. It has since become a major holiday centre, especially in self-catering, to the amazement of the local population, who were previously dependent almost entirely on the local fishing industry. The pace of life remains doggedly slow, and tourists who expect fast service and fast repairs will be quickly disillusioned. Anticipation has no place in the Algarve: someone who does not ask for the bill in a restaurant does not want it yet, the waiter will assume. If a car, refrigerator or heating system has not actually broken down, then it will be assumed to be in perfect working order. This is part of the charm of the Portuguese way of life in the provinces, and the sooner holiday-makers get used to it the more relaxed and enjoyable will be their stay.

The Algarve consists of a series of predominantly quiet, unsophisticated resorts on a coast that offers more than a hundred miles of superb beaches and breathtaking views. But these do not extend to the border town of **Vila Real de Santo Antonio,** once sober and stately, now noisy and brash in high season. Its principal advantage is its proximity to Spain, ten minutes away by ferry over the Guadiana River, which is clearly visible from some modern apartments on the Portuguese bank. Unfortunately, the nearest beach is a considerable walk, at the mouth of the Guadiana. West of the town is the vibrant resort of **Monte Gordo,** with a much superior sandy beach and an active if unsophisticated nightlife including a disco and a casino. Unlike many Algarve resorts, the town stands on entirely level ground. Self-catering accommodation, all quite close to the sea, ranges from high-rise apartments to substantial villas backed by pine woods.

Westwards, the countryside is flat and uninteresting, and the artificial holiday centre built at **Altura** reflects its surroundings. **Tavira** is elegant and most attractive, situated on the river Gilão and off the tourist track. It also has a fine beach on Tavira island, a short distance by ferry. Unfortunately, a nearby development, beside a road leading to the village of **Cabanas,** is dreary and claustrophobic, with a beach that disappears at high tide. To the south-west are the thriving fishing villages of **Fuzeta,** very tiny, with a few scattered villas, and **Olhão,** whose maze of whitewashed houses has scarcely changed since the days of Moorish occupation. Self-catering accommodation here is hard to find, but Olhão provides access by ferry to two delightful islands. **Armona,** just 15 minutes away, has two superb beaches, one of which, facing the mainland, is probably the warmest in Portugal and ideal for children. The rapid increase in self-catering apartments here will inevitably begin to spoil the atmosphere for some. **Culatra,** 45 minutes from Olhão, is discouraging major development but has a number of apartments, some indifferently constructed. The ferry does not run after dark, so your nightlife on the mainland has to last until dawn.

 Faro, the capital of the province, has the odd apartment to rent in the charming old quarter, but the ambience quickly disappears in its ill-conceived concrete suburbs. The fishing port is now an up-market yacht marina. Faro's beaches and self-catering accommodation are at **Praia de Faro,** a sandy island (really a peninsula) west of the city. It is hugely overcrowded in season and suffers from aircraft noise. Inland, north of Faro, a number of towns and villages have a good selection of villas to rent. **Santa Barbara de Nexe** is untroubled by mass tourism and is relaxed and rural, surrounded by hills; the sea is 30 minutes' drive. **Estoi** has the same agreeable landscape but it is much less attractive. **Bordeira** is a small village with a few houses. Close by, standing side by side, **Quinta das Raposeiras** and **Quinta da Holanda** were created entirely for the purpose of self-catering in a nonetheless tasteful development, with fine views of the sea, also some half an hour away by car.

 Further west along the coast, **Vale do Lobo** is an equally artificial but sleek estate of white villas and apartments, many of extremely high quality, spread across

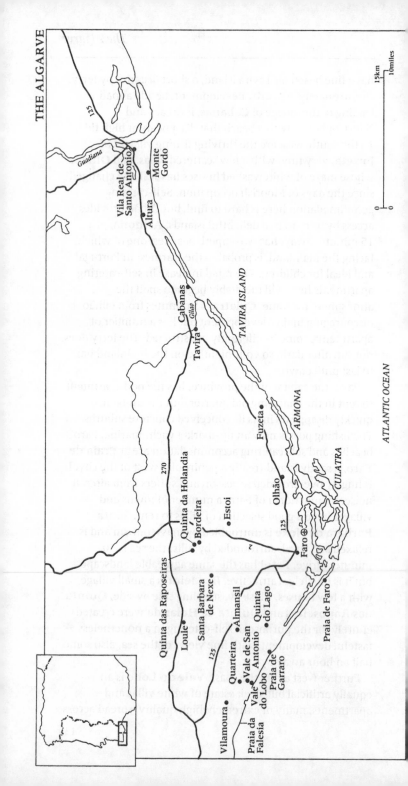

THE ALGARVE

ATLANTIC OCEAN

Guadiana

Gilão

TAVIRA ISLAND

ARMONA

CULATRA

15km
10miles

Vila Real de Santo António
Monte Gordo
Altura
Cabanas
Tavira
Fuzeta
Olhão
Faro
Praia de Faro

125
270
125
2

Quinta da Holandia
Bordeira
Estoi
Quinta das Raposeiras
Santa Barbara de Nexe
Loule
Almansil
Quarteira
Vale de San Antonio
Quinta do Lago
Praia de Garraro
Vale do Lobo
Vilamoura
Praia da Falesia

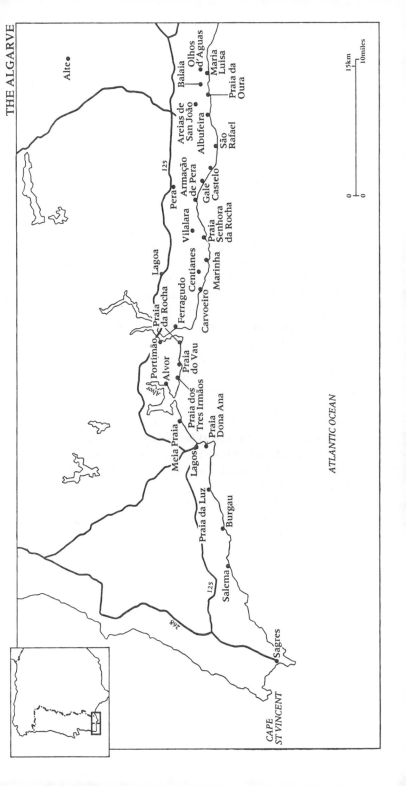

THE ALGARVE

Alte

Olhos d'Aguas
Balaia
Maria Luisa
Praia da Oura
Areias de San João
Albufeira
São Rafael
Pera
Armação de Pera
Gale
Castelo
Vilalara
Praia Senhora da Rocha
Centianes
Lagoa
Marinha
Praia da Rocha
Ferragudo
Carvoeiro
Portimão
Alvor
Praia do Vau
Alvor
Praia dos Tres Irmãos
Praia Dona Ana
Meia Praia
Lagos
Praia da Luz
Burgau
Salema
Sagres

125

268

ATLANTIC OCEAN

CAPE
ST VINCENT

0   15km
0   10miles

more than a thousand acres. Its western edge backs on to a demanding golf course, one of many sports facilities here. Other parts of the development are still growing, so any visitors without cars are heavily dependent on the shuttle bus service to visit the nightclub and the half a dozen restaurants. The supermarket is also a long way from any villas near the sea.

Vale do Lobo has a superb sandy beach, unlike its smaller neighbouring development, **Vale de San Antonio,** which has no beach at all: the sea is at least a mile away. **Praia do Garrão** is less of a resort than a smart residential area, with many well-appointed villas and a fine beach. It is used by most holiday-makers based slightly inland at **Almansil,** which has some good houses owned by the substantial expatriate British population, and an aquatic amusement park with a giant water-slide. Back on the coast, **Quinta do Lago,** an up-market enclave (1700 acres) facing a secluded and sheltered inlet, often seems full of celebrities in dark glasses trying desperately hard to be noticed. The 24-hour security is obtrusive.

Further west, **Quarteira** gives the appearance of an overspill from the Spanish Costas, with high-rise, run-down apartments, tasteless snack bars and a dingy appearance. Even the nightlife is limited, and near the port the beach suffers from traffic noise and some pollution. The few villas available are at the back of the town, up a steep hill.

Continuing west, **Vilamoura** is a major self-catering centre, with several miles of apartment blocks and separate houses. The best apartment accommodation is centred on the yachting marina, but even here the complex is unfinished and threatening to become shabby ahead of its time. The casino and most of the shops, bars and restaurants lie conveniently close. The untidy main beach, east of the marina, lacks charm and can be overcrowded in summer. Two miles inland, another series of high-rise apartments mars rolling countryside around a separate development, rescued partly by some attractive villas standing on the old golf course. Visitors complain that the shuttle bus service linking the outlying areas to the centre is unreliable.

Inland, about 30 minutes from Vilamoura, there are many villas close to **Loulé,** a bustling market town famed for its local handicraft industry. British holiday-makers pining for their animals have the perfect excursion here: a dogs' home. For those with little interest in a beach holiday, a few houses are available near **Alte,** a genuine and so far unspoilt village but a good hour and a half north from the coast by a circuitous route.

East of Vilamoura, **Praia de Falesia** has recently made an effort to improve its facilities, but is essentially just a sheltered stretch of beach. **Olhos d'Aguas** is a fishing village fast losing its identity through the sheer weight of visitors; but the sandy beach, sheltered by rocks, will appeal to many. **Balaia** has a number of thriving restaurants whose principal clientele come from the nearby apartments. **Maria Luisa,** with a mixture of hotels and flats, has few amenities but an attractive beach. All these places are within easy reach of **Albufeira,** the largest resort on the Algarve, and also the busiest and the noisiest, with a vigorous nightlife. Paradoxically, the original Moorish fishing village, which defiantly still functions, has a charming old quarter, full of cobbled streets. A tunnel gives access to the beach, extremely attractive but hopelessly inadequate for the press of humanity that arrives in high summer.

Self-catering in Albufeira proper consists largely of apart-hotels – apartments run by local hotels, combining some of the worst features of both. But much of the self-catering accommodation featured in holiday brochures as Albufeira is in fact outside the town. The closest, in **Areias de Sao João,** a suburb to the east up a steep hill, can take 20 minutes to reach by bus or car in season because of traffic jams. San João is served by the beach area of **Praia da Oura,** very much reminiscent of the large Spanish resorts, swamped by high-rise apartments and facilities where price, not quality, is the key. The beach, though splendid, is too small for the number of visitors who use it in July and August. Holiday-makers with a car would be better advised to go west of Albufeira to **São Rafael, Castelo** or **Gale,** lovely beaches with little local restaurants but few other amenities. There are houses to rent behind the beach and near **Pera,** an inland village with winding cobbled streets.

Further west, **Armação de Pera** has one of the longest beaches in the Algarve, backed by cliffs and a tree-lined promenade with exotic plants. The original village is now dwarfed by a row of ugly apartment blocks, and the resort has plunged down-market, with hamburger restaurants and British pubs. More discriminating visitors can pretend it does not exist by keeping themselves to themselves at nearby **Vilalara,** an exclusive and expensive estate.

Good-quality villas are also available near the delightful coves of **Praia Senhora da Rocha, Marinha** and **Centianes,** west of the town. As there is no coast road, the inland rural town of **Lagoa,** noted for its local wines, provides the gateway to **Carvoeiro.** Self-catering apartments and villas have transformed Carvoeiro from a secluded village at the end of a bumpy track to a smart resort. For the moment it still keeps its charm and genuine Portuguese atmosphere; but high-rise development is creeping in, part tower block, part whitewashed cubes on the cliffs. The beach, which has a vibrant disco, is sheltered but far from substantial.

From Lagoa the road continues westwards to **Portimão,** a fishing port on the Alvor river, noted for its cheap quayside restaurants with, unusually for Portugal, swift service. As all the traffic must funnel through a single main road, jams can reach epic proportions in summer, and no one should seriously consider renting a flat in the centre. Accommodation is available just six or seven minutes away by water-taxi on the far side of the river, in the unspoilt village of **Ferragudo,** an outstanding water-sports centre, with beaches, restaurants and bars.

Praia da Rocha, on the coast, is growing in size and declining in sophistication, with expensive restaurants and nightclubs alongside cheap discos and fast-food joints. If you can negotiate the steep steps, it has what many regard as the best beach in Portugal, unrelenting golden sand backed by rugged cliffs. At the eastern end, however, towering apartment blocks (now largely complete) ensure that the beach will be swamped in summer. Try instead

Praia do Vau, at the quieter, if rockier, western end of the beach: it has some convenient villa accommodation nearby.

Alvor, westwards along the coast, has managed to keep the feel of an authentic fishing port, with the odd sailors' spit-and-sawdust bar, because there's little accommodation in the village itself: outside the village, tower blocks continue to rise, bleak outcrops in a bleaker landscape. The Torralta self-catering complex is close to the best beach, **Praia dos Tres Irmãos,** rocky and sheltered.

Lagos, a fine old historic town overrun by tourists in midsummer, is the focal-point of many nearby villas. Try to find one near **Praia Dona Ana,** a sheltered beach to the south-west. Most apartment accommodation lies close to the large eastern beach of **Meia Praia,** which has good fish restaurants but is otherwise rather overwhelming.

West of Lagos, all the immediate resorts cater primarily for self-catering. **Salema** has a large beach overlooked by villas and apartments, most of them in a self-contained complex opposite the cobbled, sloping streets of the original fishing village. **Praia da Luz,** once a peaceful hamlet, is now a growing villa development with excellent sports facilities. **Burgau,** with its fishermen's cottages around a sheltered horseshoe-shaped bay, has lovely sands, a growing number of villas, but little nightlife. It is much more difficult to obtain self-catering accommodation in **Sagres,** still for most of the year a sleepy but atmospheric fishing port, but well worth the effort. Between Sagres and Cape St Vincent, with the most powerful lighthouse in Europe, are many delightful little sandy beaches, although the sea is frequently rough and the currents dangerous.

Getting there

Despite recent improvements, Faro airport is unable to cope adequately with the volume of holiday-makers passing through at peak periods. Whatever the local representatives of tour operators may say, British visitors on their way home are well advised not to go through passport control without first satisfying

145

themselves that their aircraft has actually landed, as facilities airside are inadequate for a long wait. Assume the worst: take drinks and snacks with you. If you are returning a hire car, retain it until you have a clear idea of any flight delays; if your aircraft is still in the UK, you can safely take a trip to the beach.

Charter flights go to Faro from a variety of UK airports during the summer months, but they are almost all oversubscribed.

From Bristol, Cardiff, Gatwick, Luton and Stansted the flight to Faro takes 2¾ hours; from Birmingham, East Midlands and Manchester 3 hours; from Glasgow and Newcastle 3¼ hours.

By car, Lisbon is nearly 1300 miles from Calais and more than 1150 miles from Cherbourg, by way of Bordeaux and Salamanca. This arduous journey can be shortened by using the Plymouth–Santander ferry, which normally involves travelling overnight, but even from here the onward route via Salamanca involves one overnight stop if you are driving to Lisbon, possibly two to Lagos and the Algarve, and all the route is on non-motorway roads. Unless you are a fanatical motorist, or have a very long holiday, the return journey to the Algarve must therefore be ruled out on the basis of the time it takes.

French Motorail is available daily in summer between Paris and Lisbon, where after an overnight journey passengers have a day for sightseeing before their car (which travels separately) arrives.

Local transport

Car hire remains comparatively cheap on the Algarve because of the number of local firms competing for business. Check prices and the prospective vehicle carefully before committing yourself.

The Algarve railway line provides about eight trains a day between Lagos and the Spanish border; the journey takes 2½ hours but is of little scenic interest. Lagos, Portimão, Albufeira and Faro are the principal bus termini and there are regular local services.

Weather

Averages	Jan	Feb	Mar	Apr	May	Jun
Temperature	61	61	63	68	72	76
Sun hours	5	6	7	8	10	12
Rainy days	9	9	11	6	4	1
Sea temp.	59	59	59	61	63	66

Weather *continued*

Averages	Jul	Aug	Sep	Oct	Nov	Dec
Temperature	82	82	79	76	66	62
Sun hours	12	11	9	7	5	5
Rainy days	0	0	2	5	8	9
Sea temp.	70	70	70	68	64	61

Rain is extremely rare in July and August, when the temperatures are reduced by sea breezes. Dry, sunny summers inevitably give way to unsettled, much cooler winters, when rain is always a possibility.

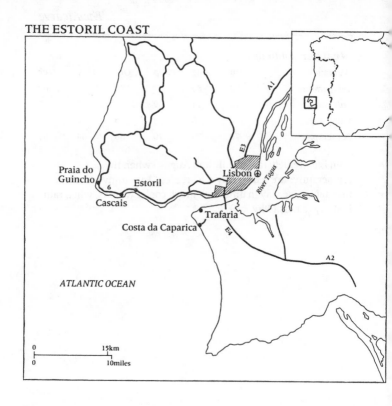

The Estoril coast

Many residents abandon **Lisbon** for the seaside in the
hottest months, leaving their houses locked and empty.
A few sometimes advertise their properties for rent in a
rather quaint magazine called *Anglo-Portuguese News*.
Obtaining the current issue of the magazine in good time
in the UK can be a problem, but more adventurous
holiday-makers, especially those without children, have
been known to book a hotel for the first few nights in order
to find a Lisbon house or apartment for the remainder of
their stay.

Accommodation in the lower part of the city, the
commercial centre known as the Baixa, risks being stuffy
and noisy. Below the castle, the Alfama, or old quarter, has

148

a marvellous ambience, but most houses and flats are dingy and poorly equipped. Barrio Alta, the upper town, has much better quality houses and is well positioned for the nightlife, especially the *fado* restaurants, where the *fadista* sings the haunting songs that capture both the indecision and the melancholy of the Portuguese attitude to life. Houses further out, close to the fine gardens of the Parque Eduardo VII, are coveted and difficult to come by.

Lisbon has no beach, but there are four resorts nearby, all with self-catering accommodation. The most popular is **Costa da Caparica,** more than 15 miles of sand-dunes, across the River Tagus. An hourly ferry from the riverside suburb of Belem runs to Trafaria, only a mile from Caparica by bus. This is a lively resort, overwhelmingly Portuguese in character, with only a sprinkling of foreign tourists. The restaurants are excellent and the bars stay open late. A railway runs along the dunes in summer.

Caparica does not suffer from pollution, which is more than can be said for **Estoril** where bathing cannot be recommended. An electric train runs every few minutes from Lisbon's Cais do Sodre to what was once among Europe's most chic resorts. The old gambling clientele has now disappeared, leaving Estoril with an almost redundant casino that is somehow symbolic: echoes of grandeur but no real substance. While its back streets are quiet and its gardens meticulously manicured, you have to cross an extremely dangerous main road and use the tunnels under the railway line to gain access to the beach. Most of the villas available to rent are located on the hills above the town, surrounded by pine trees.

Two miles further west, **Cascais** retains a little of its original character as a fishing port, with narrow lanes and fine old mansions, some turned into flats. It, too, suffers from pollution, spoiling an otherwise attractive main beach, sandy and sheltered. Traffic here is a serious problem in summer, especially at weekends. The best area in which to stay is close to the pedestrian precinct.

As the coast road swings north, Cascais gives way to **Praia do Guincho,** a sweeping bay of sand, punctuated by jagged rocks. Some of the houses to rent have a fine view

149

of the Atlantic rollers which, together with a fierce undercurrent, keep Guincho clear of pollution but make it a very dangerous place at which to swim.

Getting there

To Lisbon from Gatwick or Luton (2½ hours); from Manchester (2¾ hours). Lisbon's Portela airport is 4½ miles north of the city.

Local transport

A hire car is not necessary in Lisbon, as the public transport system is excellent, especially the trams (*electricos*), for which blocks (*modulos*) of tickets can be purchased in advance at the major railway termini.

Weather

Averages	Jan	Feb	Mar	Apr	May	Jun
Temperature	57	59	63	68	70	77
Sun hours	5	7	7	9	10	11
Rainy days	6	6	7	4	2	1
Sea temp.	59	57	57	59	63	64

Averages	Jul	Aug	Sep	Oct	Nov	Dec
Temperature	81	82	81	70	63	59
Sun hours	12	12	9	7	6	5
Rainy days	0	0	3	7	6	7
Sea temp.	68	68	68	66	63	59

The Estoril coast, which has more than 3000 hours of sunshine each year, is among the sunniest parts of Europe. Its sunshine and air and sea temperatures compare very favourably with those of the Algarve.

Spain

Spain offers a wide range of self-catering accommodation and cheap charter flights, enabling rental companies, tour operators and enterprising travellers to construct holidays that can be remarkable value for money. Self-catering holidays in Spain are significantly cheaper than their equivalents in France and often cheaper than those in Italy or Portugal. But the old adage that you get what you pay for still applies to the Spanish Costas and to the Balearic Islands. Accommodation provided at extremely low prices will almost certainly have major disadvantages, in a country where the Spanish construction industry has turned cutting corners into an art in itself.

At the top end of the market, Spain has a substantial number of villas set in their own grounds with private swimming-pools. Some of the best are to be found on the Costa del Sol and on the islands of Majorca and Ibiza. All have maid service and the more expensive may come with a cook.

In the next category are villas located on specially constructed estates, often near a golf course, reflecting that this is a major attraction for many holiday-makers. In most cases these villas have a shared swimming-pool, or a large communal swimming-pool often part of a central complex with restaurants, shops and play areas. Some, especially on the Costa del Sol, form part of a specially constructed marina, but others may lie a few miles inland.

More modest villas without a pool can be found along the whole length of the Costas and especially in Majorca and Minorca, whose *'urbinaçion'*, or purpose-built estate, its streets laid out in symmetrical lines, can be seen all around the islands and has been copied elsewhere. Some developments with shared gardens and swimming-pools consist of rows of smart terraced houses: some have spacious, well-equipped bungalows and apartments around a central pool.

On the Costa del Sol, Majorca and Ibiza, many modern developments have been styled on the Moorish *pueblos*, with shaded courtyards, arches and little gardens, usually a mix of small houses and apartments on the ground and first floor.

Property away from the coast is more difficult to find. Many small villages within half an hour's drive of the sea do have houses or apartments to rent in summer, but they rarely appear in any of the holiday brochures. Such a property may be an older house, modernised and divided into flats, and you may need to know a British family with their own property nearby to establish the right kind of contacts.

Heating, unnecessary on the Costa del Sol, is often highly desirable for out-of-season holidays elsewhere on the Costas. While most large apartment blocks have a central hot water tank, other apartments and practically all villas rely on butane (*butano*) gas cylinders. Most kitchens are designed with a large cupboard under the sink to accommodate them. There are strict regulations: the storage area for gas cylinders must have adequate ventilation, and the boiler they supply must have a proper flue. Even so, tourist authorities recommend that the water heater be turned off at night and a window left open whenever the boiler is in use.

In or out of season, the high-rise apartments available at all the major Spanish resorts have little to commend them. Some are apart-hotels with a communal swimming-pool and poolside bar and sometimes a restaurant. Half board is often available, with either lunch or dinner, and perhaps on a 14-night holiday the option to mix half board with self-catering. What they invariably lack is any kind of room service.

In both apart-hotels and straightforward apartments, the kitchen or kitchenette is invariably a very small area, often simply an alcove, not segregated from the main living area. Cooking smells therefore may linger and be a particular problem if the same space is used for sleeping in at night.

The smallest apartments are called studios, effectively bed-sitting-rooms with convertible bed-settees. Where the studio is taken by a group of three, one person may find that the third bed is a camp bed because there is insufficient room for anything more comfortable.

Expect sparse furnishings and the minimum of equipment in these studios: there will be no dishwasher, and most refrigerators will not have a freezer compartment. Leaving a huge pile of dishes for the maid on her weekly or twice-weekly visit is also unlikely to be successful.

Most apartments offered by holiday companies are registered with the local tourist association, so it is possible to check whether it matches the description in the brochure. Some 90,000 flats have been classified by the associations into grades represented by up to four keys.

● **Four keys: Luxury** A block of high-quality construction in an attractive location, with lift if of more than two floors, service lift, rubbish disposal facilities on each floor, private parking, constant hot water, air-conditioning, telephone, separate kitchen, two bathrooms where the apartment sleeps more than four persons.

● **Three keys: First class** A block of high-quality construction, lift if of more than three floors, private parking, constant hot water, central heating, telephone link to porter, two bathrooms where the apartment sleeps more than five persons.

● **Two keys: Second class** A block of good-quality construction, lift if of more than three floors, telephone link to porter from each floor, hot water and heating available, two bathrooms where the apartment sleeps more than five persons.

● **One key: Third class** A lift if the block is of more than four floors, hot water heater in each apartment, two bathrooms where the apartment sleeps more than six persons.

As a result of hard-earned experience, the owners of apartment blocks or their representatives tend to take the inventory of equipment in each flat seriously and to check it on departure. Under Spanish law they are entitled to ask for a deposit of up to 25 per cent of the total weekly rental price of the flat as security against breakages and damage to furniture and equipment. If you sign an inventory as correct on your arrival, you cannot change your mind later, so your own check on the state of the equipment and furnishings should be as methodical as that of the owner's representative. Against this, registration rules require the price of your stay to include the full cost of local taxes, water, electricity, gas, linen, rubbish collection and use of communal facilities.

Arrival and departure times are less flexible in Spain than they are in other countries. Unless your rental company has agreed to a special arrangement, such as making the booking for a day early to coincide with your arrival after a night flight, occupancy usually begins at 5 p.m. on the first day and ends at noon on the last. This may mean that you have a hot day ahead of you before you can take possession of your apartment if your flight lands early in the morning. It is not advisable to overstay your welcome, either. The management of apartment blocks is empowered to charge three times the daily price of the apartment for each day or part of a day of illegal occupancy, and it can also cut off all the amenities, including electricity and water; some managements have been known to do so.

The electricity supply in Spain is being standardised at 200 or 225 volts, which is suitable for UK appliances. A number of older buildings still use 110 or 125 volts, though most apartment blocks in tourist areas have already been converted.

What to take with you

Unless you are travelling to Spain by French Motorail, or your destination is just across the border on the Costa Brava, you will be restricted in what you can take with you on a charter or scheduled flight. Fortunately, linen is provided and changed at least once a week in the great majority of Spanish apartments and villas. Towels are also provided, but they will probably not be ideal for bathing or sunbathing, so take some of your own.

There is little prospect of Spanish accommodation, other than the most luxurious, possessing a kettle or a teapot; tea-bags will also usually be of an inferior quality, and more expensive.

Spanish electrical appliances are also suspect: take a portable iron if you want to use one as you may find any iron provided heavy and cumbersome.

If you are travelling by car with fewer luggage restrictions, other items can be added. Although most villas will be adequately furnished, assume the worst and take a bottle-opener, tin-opener, corkscrew, matches, candles (short power cuts are common in Spain), soap, coat-hangers, tea-towels, cleaning materials, refuse bags and a sharp kitchen knife. You may also come to appreciate a pair of pliers for emergency repairs, an adjustable spanner for connecting cooking-gas bottles, a torch with new batteries and a set of small screwdrivers.

Take enough film for your camera to last the entire holiday. Film, developing and printing are nearly always more expensive in Spain. Sometimes out-of-date film is sold in markets, and cut-price printing promoted that produces inferior results.

Eating in

Throughout Spain, the bakery (*panaderia*) is often the first shop to open, at around 7 a.m., and the first to close, when the bread has all been sold. The *panadero* bakes every day except Sunday. Each region has its own shape and type of bread, which is sold at government-controlled prices. Some bakers are large enough to include a *pasteleria*, or pastry shop, with a vast selection of wonderful cakes and pastries. Try *huevo hilado*, spun egg whites with sugar.

The greengrocer (*verduleria*) sells by the kilogramme, and customers generally make their own selection. Much of the produce is cheaper, though not necessarily of better quality, at a market. The municipal market (*mercado*) in large towns is often a grand, domed hall open every day from 8 to 2 (except Sundays and public holidays). Village markets are more likely to be on a weekly basis and much less well organised. Both will have a great deal of fruit, which in Spain is sold almost literally everywhere: on the roadside, in bars, by private citizens out of their front parlour. The formal fruiterer's (*fruteria*) is comparatively rare, but more likely to have fresh fruit in winter, imported from the Canary Islands.

For fresh fish, visit the fish market, which is usually in a separate building to the main market. It will open at the same time, around 8 a.m., but will close when all the produce is sold out. As Spanish fishermen rarely go to sea on Sundays, fresh fish is generally not available on Mondays. The fishmonger's (*pescaderia*) is more likely to have expensive fish such as sole (*lenguado*) or deep-sea prawns (*langostinos*).

The butcher (*carniceria*) may have what seems an empty shop, especially in summer: the meat is kept in a fridge, and the butcher sells from a coloured chart showing the various cuts. He will bring out only what you choose on the chart, which should also carry a list of prices. The best beef (*carne de vaca*) and veal (*carne de ternera*) come from the north, where the climate is cooler and the grass greener. Lamb (*cordero*) is generally a more reliable purchase, especially on the Costa del Sol, where beef is expensive or tough – sometimes both. Poultry (*polleria*) is sometimes sold in a specialist shop as well as at the butcher's shop and comes with innards, head and feet unless you indicate otherwise.

Other than fresh pork which is available at the butcher's, all pork products are sold at the *charcuteria*. When the delicatessen becomes more of an up-market grocer's, it is known as a *mantequeria*. Goods at the lower end of the market, including cooking oil, wine, bread and cheaper tinned foodstuffs, are sold in a general store known as *comestibles*, often arranged as a self-service supermarket.

Larger supermarkets (*supermercados*) have been built on the edge of larger resorts in the Costas to meet tourists' demands. They are usually much cheaper than individual specialist shops. Table wine such as Rioja or Valdepeñas are the best value, unless you visit a village *bodega* to taste and buy wine from the barrel.

Eating out

The earlier you eat lunch or dinner, the less appetising your meal is likely to be. This is because only restaurants in major resorts catering primarily for tourists have adjusted their hours to suit the holiday-maker, and these restaurants serve bland, anonymous dishes. If you want to eat genuine Spanish cuisine, resign yourself to the fact that lunch will not be served before 1.30 p.m., and no self-respecting Spaniard will sit down for dinner before 9.30 p.m. The only way to be sure of a good meal is to eat late, and to eat in a restaurant crammed with Spaniards.

Restaurants are graded into five categories, indicated by one to five forks. Very few of them display their category clearly, in some instances because the category affects the prices they are permitted to charge. The number of forks is determined by the surroundings, not by the quality of the food.

By law, every restaurant must display its prices, which include taxes and sometimes a service charge. They are also obliged to offer a set-price meal called the *menu del dia*, which includes a quarter-litre of house wine per person. Many restaurants will also offer a series of *platos combinados*, a variable and more modest set meal usually consisting of soup with roll, a main dish without vegetables, followed by coffee.

Bars serve sandwiches, other snacks and *tapas*, which are plates of olives, nuts and various sliced delicacies. *Tapas* are usually placed on your table automatically when you order a drink, but will then be added to your bill – at one time they were free. Bars specialising in *tapas* are called *tascas*. *Ventas* are roadside restaurants, offering slightly higher comfort that the traditional British roadside café and infinitely superior food.

Cafeterias should not be confused with the self-service establishments common in the UK. In reality they are small restaurants where customers have the option of a faster (but rarely cheaper) meal by sitting at the bar. *Merenderos* are beach restaurants specialising in fish, but also offering simple meals such as an omelette, chips and salad. *Fondas*, modest inns found in the backstreets of towns, offer not only a bed for the night but a number of outstanding set dishes at reasonable prices.

Wherever you choose to eat, the key to good service lies in summoning the waiter with a mixture of confidence and tact. Address him as 'señor' and beckon him using all your fingers, palm downwards: attempts to signal him using fewer fingers can be misinterpreted as a rude gesture.

Children

Spanish children still take the siesta largely abandoned by their parents. In consequence, it is by no means unusual to see even eight- or nine-year-olds alert and tucking into a large meal in a restaurant late at night or running around in the early hours of the morning. Taking your children to a restaurant in Spain, other than perhaps the most elegant, presents no problems . . . other than that they may not like the food. But most restaurants can provide undemanding meals, such as chicken and chips followed by ice-cream (*helado*). Self-catering for children is simplified by the large variety of frozen convenience meals available in hypermarkets and supermarkets, including hamburgers, pizzas and the inevitable fish fingers.

If you are travelling by car, it is considerably less trouble to take a baby's necessities with you for the entire stay, including nappies and baby food. Buying items for babies in Spain can be expensive and time-consuming outside main resort areas. Environmentally friendly nappies are not widely available in Spain. Instant baby food is available in huge quantities in supermarkets, but there are subtle differences in taste between apparently identical Continental and UK products, and not all babies adjust easily.

The Spanish have a natural affection for children, and any danger to them in Spain is much more likely to come from other foreigners. It is prudent to keep all children away from animals. In Spain the sun is a serious hazard to children. Babies should be kept out of the sun as much as possible and small children encouraged to wear shirts and hats.

Transport

Spain has an extensive rail network, but visitors electing to travel by rail should appreciate that the principal mainline route from London, crossing the Spanish frontier at Port-Bou north of Barcelona, hugs the Costas coastline only as far as Valencia. Destinations further south, such as Benidorm, either require you to use a local service or, such as Malaga, run on routes out of Madrid where you must change stations. In Spain, there is almost always a mad rush at ticket offices, because the one window (*venta immediata*) selling the ticket you want is invariably open only 30 minutes before the train is due to depart. You can avoid the problem, but at a price: if you buy a ticket from the *venta anticipada* window more than two hours before a train's departure, you must travel (or, at any event, pay for) a minimum distance. This varies according to the type of train. On the luxurious, air-conditioned *Talgo*, it is 155 miles; on *Electrotrenes* or TER trains, 125 miles; and on express or *Rapido* trains, which usually go long distances overnight, 75 miles. Avoid wherever possible *semi-directos* or *tranvias* trains, which are slow short-haul services; and be warned that the mail train or *correo* will find stations to stop at that are too small even to appear on a map.

Many villages, especially on the Costa de Almeria, are nonetheless accessible only by bus. They are cheap and reliable, usually operating a local network from the main town or towns in each province. Services on Sundays and public holidays are drastically reduced, but Saturday is regarded as a normal working day for transport purposes. The biggest problem is often finding from where a bus leaves, as many towns do not possess a main bus station.

Avoiding problems

Severe sunburn is a danger in all parts of Spain, but especially in the south. Sunscreen lotions are widely available but not necessarily those with the highest filter factors. Adults with a fair or sensitive skin may find that they need to start with the highest factor (15) for a few days, to obtain virtually complete protection, and to work downwards to a medium factor (6, say). Lotions need to be re-applied regularly and particularly after swimming.

After sunburn, upset stomachs and diarrhoea are the most common problems. The single most probable cause is not food poisoning but the extravagant use of oil and garlic in Spanish cooking. You can ask a restaurant to prepare a meal without garlic (*sin ajo*), and for meat to be roasted in the oven (*al homo/asado*) or grilled (*à la parrilla*). If you have a sensitive stomach, avoid alcohol and fried foods. Most restaurants will bring boiled potatoes (*patatas cocidas*) instead of chips even if they are not on the menu.

Restaurants, villa complexes and petrol stations are all required by law to keep a complaints book (*hoja de reclamacion*), which is regularly inspected by the authorities. Even asking for the book often concentrates the proprietor's mind on resolving your complaint, as large fines can be, and often are, imposed on establishments whose products or services fail to meet standards.

A complaints form can also be obtained from any official

tourist information office. It should be completed and posted, together with any supporting evidence, to the regional tourist department (the tourist office will provide the address) before you leave Spain. Do not expect to receive any compensation, except where the dispute relates to a bill: even then, the authorities will not consider any complaint unless the bill has been previously paid in full. Although credit and charge cards are widely accepted in Spain, some establishments have a quite low maximum limit irrespective of the cardholder's personal limit. This can cause problems at, for example, a villa or apartment complex with credit facilities where the holiday-maker intends to settle his account at the end of the holiday.

Protecting your credit cards and other valuables is a major hassle in Spain, where street and beach crime and burglaries are common. Take sensible precautions.

There are no national numbers for emergencies requiring ambulance or fire services, but either the national (091) or municipal (092) police may be able to assist through their 24-hour emergency service.

Opening hours

Banks are usually open from 9 to 1 but close an hour earlier in summer. Shops' opening hours are half an hour on either side of 9.30 to 1.30 and 5.30 to 8.30 from Monday to Friday, although major department stores in large towns stay open in the afternoon, a good time to visit them. Most shops close on Saturday afternoons and all day on Sunday, with the exception of bakers and some supermarkets, which are open on Sunday mornings.

Public holidays

1 January (New Year's Day); **6 January** (Epiphany or Twelfth Night, the evening in Spain when children receive their Christmas presents); **Good Friday; Easter Sunday; 1 May** (Labour Day); **Corpus Christi** (variable); **24 June** (St John's Day); **29 June** (Day of St Peter and St Paul); **25 July** (*Santiago*, the Day of St James, the patron saint of Spain); **15 August** (Feast of the Assumption of the Virgin Mary); **12 October** (Hispanic Day, when Columbus discovered the Americas); **1 November** (All Saints' Day); **8 December** (Feast of the Immaculate Conception); **25 December** (Christmas Day).

What to bring back

Leather goods: coats, shoes,
    handbags, wallets, belts
Wrought ironwork
Brassware
Stone ornaments
Pottery
Hand-made jewellery
Carpets
Rugs
Traditional costumes
Modern fashion goods
    (Spanish designer labels)

Tour operators

For details see page 213

Aer Lingus Holidays
Airlink Holidays
Airtours
Albir Travel
Allans Holidays
Allegro Holidays
Astbury Apartments
Avon Europe
Beach Villas
Blakes Holidays
Brits Abroad
Burstin Travel
Cabo Roig Villas &
    Apartments
Cala d'Or Villas
Casa International Holidays
Castaways
Catalan Villas
Celtic Line Travel
City Cruiser Holidays
Club Cantabrica
Club Pollensa Holidays
Continental Villas
Cornisa Travel and Villas
Cosmos
Costa Blanca Holiday
Crystal Holiday
Denia Holidays
DSI Services (Nerja)
Espan Apartments

Estartit Owners' Club
European Villas
Exclusive Javea Villas
Executive Villas
Falcoln de-Luxe Resorts
Fencott Barnes International
Fincasol Holidays
Forest Downs Investments
Freelance Holidays
Geoff Williamson Travel
Global Air Holidays
Hamilton Holidays
Hartland Holidays
Holmes Travel
Horizon Holidays
Impact Holidays
Indamar Apartments
Intasun Holidays
Interhome
Jean Harper Holidays
Kent Travel Service
Lancaster Holidays
Magic of Spain
Majorca Apartments & Villas
Marshall Sutton
Martyn Holidays
Memories Travel
Menco
Meon Travel
Mojacar Holidays
Mojacar Villas
NAT Holidays
Now Holidays and Travel
OSL
The Owners' Syndicate
Palm Luxury Villas
Palmer & Parker Holidays
Paloma Holidays
Panorama Holiday Group
Paramount Holidays
Patricia Wildblood
Pleasurewood Holidays
Premier Property Services
R & R Travel Services
Realcare Villa Services
Redwing Holidays
RentaVilla
Roc Villas

Saga Holidays	Tarleton Travel
San Clemente Villas	Thomson Holidays
Sealink Holidays	Tjaerborg
Seasun Tentrek	Villa Select
Select Holidays	Villa Service
SFV Holidays	Villacana Villas
Something Special Travel	Villas España Holidays
Spanish Harbour Holidays	VillaSeekers
Starvillas	Villasun Holidays
Sunscene Holidays	VIP Villa Holidays
Sunset Villas	Walton Property Services
Sunwest Travel	Woodcock Travel

The Balearic Islands

At first sight the Balearics, lying east of Spain's
Mediterranean coastline, are not the place for a quiet and
discriminating holiday. The islands have almost one-fifth
of all Spanish self-catering accommodation and more than
4.5 million foreign visitors a year, some 750,000 in August
alone. With more than 2 million British tourists among
them, scarcely a single airport in the UK possessing
passport facilities does not have a flight to at least one of
the islands during the summer.

The Balearic authorities are now making a determined
effort to raise the quality of the accommodation and to
improve local amenities. In future, planning permission
will be given only for high-quality self-catering
development. Much more money is being invested to
improve facilities in the reduction of sea pollution, in
beach cleaning, road maintenance, street lighting and
waste disposal. The emphasis throughout the islands is to
be on quality, not quantity.

However, Majorca, Minorca, Ibiza and the tiny island of
Formentera already have a great deal more to offer than
concrete towers, dynamic discos and over-populated
beaches. By carefully choosing your villa or apartment and
hiring a car, you can escape the worst of the crowds and
sample some superb scenery.

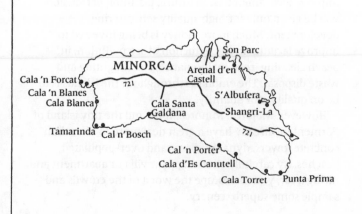

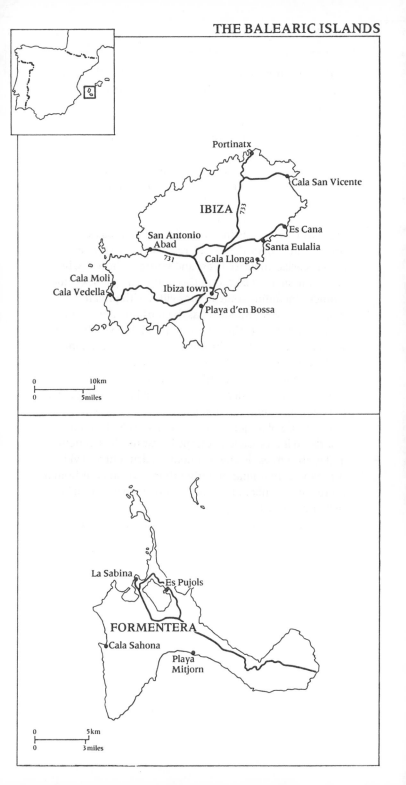

THE BALEARIC ISLANDS

IBIZA

Portinatx

Cala San Vicente

733

San Antonio Abad

Es Cana

Santa Eulalia

Cala Llonga

731

Cala Moli

Cala Vedella

Ibiza town

Playa d'en Bossa

0   10km
0   5miles

La Sabina

Es Pujols

FORMENTERA

Cala Sahona

Playa Mitjorn

0   5km
0   3 miles

The most northerly island, **Minorca,** is also the quietest. It has no large resorts reminiscent of the Spanish Costas, and despite an extensive building programme only a handful of anonymous big hotels. The nightlife is unadventurous, like most of Minorca's British visitors. Its villas and apartments, often constructed in the style of true Spanish *haciendas*, tend to be comfortable rather than luxurious. The coast is a mixture of rocks and sandy coves, sheltering tiny resorts ideal for a family holiday.

Majorca, the largest and most beautiful of the Balearics, presents two contrasting faces of tourism. It has a range of unappealing, over-developed resorts, full of concrete tower blocks, anglicised bars and saturated beaches, but also some smart self-catering accommodation in secluded hamlets, including some luxury villas with private swimming-pools. Majorca has the most to offer out of season or if the weather proves unkind: but you have to work hard for solitude during the peak summer months.

The atmosphere on Ibiza is one of complete informality, with the emphasis on youth. Holiday-makers who dislike the sight of bare flesh and the sound of brash nightlife will not be happy here. But many of Ibiza's best beaches, unlike those of Majorca, are located outside the main resorts, so it is possible to escape by car to a less frenetic and more agreeable environment. Apartment and villa complexes are utilitarian rather than luxurious, although there are a number of up-market houses patronised by the rich and famous.

The smallest and most southerly island, **Formentera,** makes neighbouring Ibiza seem large by comparison. Lacking a direct air link, and still largely undeveloped, Formentera's self-catering accommodation is simple and limited. The island is the hottest and sunniest of the Balearics.

Minorca

Those who have no option but to travel in high season can perhaps take heart from the statistic that for every ten tourists flying to Majorca, Minorca receives only one, making it the least crowded of the three major islands. Apart from a few aberrations before planning controls took effect, it has also managed to avoid the high-rise monstrosities of mainland Spain. The absence, with one or two exceptions, of giant hotels also ensures that self-catering holiday-makers are not made to feel slightly unwelcome by an industry that elsewhere still caters for mass transportation and mass entertainment.

One of the largest collections of apartments and villas overlooks the modern south-coast resort of **Cala Santa Galdana,** a magnificent curved bay of gently sloping sand. Here, unusually for Minorca, there are three substantial hotels but only one directly above the beach, which is busy but not impossibly crowded in high season. The hotels' staff are a convenient source of babysitters (tip the hall porter).

On the south-west corner of the island, **Cal 'n Bosch** and **Tamarinda** is a dual but very uninspired development of hotels and villas with two sandy beaches. Efforts have been made to eliminate suspected pollution, but the place is not recommended.

On the west coast, **Cala Blanca** has some high quality villas among pine trees behind the resort. Its principal disadvantage is its small sandy beach, hemmed in by cliffs and extremely crowded in midsummer. **Cala 'n Blanes** has a longer stretch of sand at the back of a deep bay, but most of the self-catering accommodation is the wrong side of an increasingly busy road with blind corners. **Cala 'n Forcat** consists almost entirely of a modern development of apartments around a central complex. This alone would be disproportionately large for the nearby bay, but less than 300 yards away is the massive, and ghastly, Los Delfines development, great lines of terraces of apartments stretching as far as the eye can see in an otherwise rocky and desolate wasteland; the facilities and organised entertainment will probably be extremely popular with children.

In the north-east of the island, **Son Parc** consists of a purpose-built apartment complex overlooking a broad, sandy beach, with excellent watersports facilities. Its neighbour, **Arenal d'en Castell,** is a growing resort set around a circular and, it must be said, slightly grubby bay of gently shelving sand. A road and steps lead to a series of hillside villas and apartments with no discernible centre.

Further east, **S'Albufera** lies on an inland lake and bird sanctuary, less than three miles from the fishing village of Es Grau. Its villa development, many with private swimming-pools, is sufficiently remote to make a car essential. The Albufera marshes continue towards the optimistically named **Shangri-la,** on the south side of the lake, another development of slightly higher quality houses close to a golf course.

In the far south-east, **Punta Prima** is a singularly unattractive resort. Its sandy beach is criss-crossed with seaweed and rocks and its bars and restaurants look run down and faintly seedy. **Cala Torret** is a wide, sandy beach serving a series of villa and apartment complexes, Binbeca Beach, Binbeca Torret, Bincuda, Binipark and Binivell. The best is Binivell, which has what claims (without historical support) to be the re-creation of an old Minorcan fishing village, with tiny cul-de-sacs and cobbled streets. The path to the beach is quite steep and difficult for the elderly and the very young.

Cala d'es Canutell, on the south coast, has a narrow sandy beach but practically no other amenities, and is therefore ideal for a quiet holiday. The nearest shops and restaurants are four miles away.

Cal 'n Porter ought to be a strikingly successful resort, given its attractive sandy beach and line of villas set into the cliffs above. However, many visitors come to curse the steep access to the sea, and the clifftop village lacks cohesion and any real sense of identity.

Majorca

Majorca has pinned its prosperity as a tourist centre on self-catering, which now accounts for almost 60 per cent of the total beds available. Although the island has 250 miles of coastline, for the discriminating self-catering visitor the north-west coast is much the best. At the top end of the market, elegant, isolated villas with private swimming pools can be found in three particular areas: at **Cala San Vicente,** a secluded resort with a dramatic backcloth of mountains, and a tiny beach, with dangerous currents, nestling among the rocks; on the **Formentor Peninsula,** beyond a breathtaking sequence of hairpin bends; and at **Puerto de Pollensa,** a delightful sandy bay backed by wooded hills, and a charming resort resisting the call of outright commercialism.

More modest but nonetheless well-designed villas and apartments, all good value, lie mainly just back from the beach; and new developments are planned barely within walking distance of the sea. Puerto de Pollensa's calm is shattered daily in season by the arrival of coach-loads of day-trippers from the major resorts in the south. Many self-catering holiday-makers prefer to escape to their villas until the coaches have departed.

In the north of the island but further east than Puerto de Pollensa, **Puerto de Alcudia** represents a challenge for even the skilled brochure photographer: it has a power station at the north-eastern end of the resort. The self-catering accommodation, largely apartments, is a long way from the restaurants and the shops, but is much closer to the outstanding beach, which would be more crowded were it not for the fact that many hotel visitors, faced with a long trek to the sea from the back of the town, settle for their swimming-pool instead. Alcudia is an untidy, rambling resort, almost indistinguishable in appearance from **C' an Picafort.** Half a dozen streets blemished by ugly concrete towers, their occupants deafened by all-night discos, cannot be redeemed by a long, safe, sandy beach. Most apartments at C' an Picafort are of a poor standard, and the place is not recommended.

Playa de Canamel, on the west coast, overlooked by steep wooded cliffs, offers a number of individual villas near the sea. **Cala Millor** has an agreeable beach, although the hotels have monopolised the best positions adjoining a pedestrian zone. Originally quite a sophisticated resort, it is now dominated by its discos, from where the sound carries to the equally featureless **Cala Bona.** Sea-front apartments line the coast road between the two resorts.

At the southern end of the west coast, **Cala d'Or** has much more to recommend it. Designed in Moorish style by a single architect, it consists of a series of vivid white villas and apartments clustered together around a mixture of shared and private swimming-pools. The cheapest villas are extremely good value. Many of the visitors are conspicuously affluent, patronising the up-market boutiques on the attractive main street. Unfortunately, the beach, made up of a series of tiny sandy coves, is too small to cope with the numbers in peak season. Just to the south, **Porto Petro** is fast abandoning its pretence to be a quiet fishing village, and has a number of large villas to rent. Much of the fishing fleet seems to have given way to expensive pleasure craft.

On the south coast itself, sophisticated resorts are hard to find. At the eastern end of the Bay of Palma, **El Arenal** is not the place for a quiet holiday. Its predominantly young transient population dances the night away in the local discos and is too tired during the day to notice the low-flying arrivals and departures from Palma airport. **Palma** itself, a large uninspiring city, has a number of relatively expensive apartments.

The huge twin resorts of **Palma Nova** and **Magalluf** are larger than life: full of high-rise blocks, and couples eager for fun. Discos that barely get into their stride before dawn, and a well-run casino, make up the local entertainment. Most of the apartments on offer are situated behind the hotels, some distance from the beaches, which are hopelessly overcrowded in the peak summer months.

Further west, **Paguera** is a rather disorganised town, and, like its beaches, slightly grubby in appearance. Its flats and houses lie mainly some distance from the sea, by way of some steeply rising roads. **Puerto de Soller,** on the north-west coast, has a number of apartments and houses to rent in the adjoining hills. The resort is charming at night once the thousands of summer day-trippers have departed.

Ibiza

Young couples or families with teenagers may find that Ibiza meets their aspirations in every respect. The major resorts of Ibiza town and San Antonio Abad have a spectacular nightlife that lasts from dusk to dawn, with discos that provide the ultimate sound and light experience. Some revellers will be content to stagger back to their apart-hotels to sleep off the sangria. Others will prefer to distance themselves sufficiently from the action to stay in remote villas and benefit from Ibiza's other principal attractions, watersports and sheltered beaches.

Portinatx, in the far north of Ibiza, was once evocative enough to serve as a tropical island in the film *South Pacific*. It has long since lost its desolate charm, but it remains relatively uncommercialised. Self-catering development continues to expand, mainly studio, one- and two-bedroom apartments, much of it simple but agreeably furnished. Portinatx's problem is a shortage of beaches: its three sandy stretches, of which Playa La Port is the best, are far too small for the summer population, especially as the number of visitors is multiplied by day-trippers from other parts of the island with no proper beaches at all.

The north-east resort of **Cala San Vicente** remains tiny, isolated and dominated by some unappealing hotels. Most self-catering accommodation lies some way from the beach, which shelves steeply into the sea. **Es Cana,** on the east coast, has a charming beach, set among pine trees, with extremely safe bathing. But the village is in danger of being swamped by the ever-expanding self-catering accommodation, mainly modest apartments, and the daily influx of visitors, as at Portinatx, can make it crowded.

Santa Eulalia would be an attractive resort but for its indifferent beaches, which consist mainly of rocks – and sharp rocks at that. The village centre has a promenade, a marina and an abundance of watersports, bars, restaurants and discos; but it is a considerable walk from the main self-catering centre, La Siesta. This substantial estate has apartments, bungalows and a central complex, but some visitors may find the number of steps discouraging. In the hills behind there are other self-catering developments, including some large and well-equipped villas.

Cala Llonga, further south, also has a number of fine hillside villas, some with swimming-pools; the bay is sheltered and the beach of rather unappealing greyish sand shelves gently into the sea, ideal for younger children.

Ibiza town has practically no self-catering accommodation in its attractive walled quarter, although it is occasionally possible to rent one of the imposing houses on the principal boulevards. Most modern apartments, however, are singularly lacking in comfort. Its suburb, Figueretas, has a small and grubby beach, but still better than the inhospitable rocks that border flats and bungalows along the coast. Unfortunately, no sooner does the sand emerge at **Playa d'en Bossa** in the far south than the accommodation and the beach – ironically, the best on the island – are ruined by aircraft noise. The town is directly on the flight-path from the airport, and on summer weekends you could easily imagine yourself to be at Gatwick or Heathrow.

Further west, **Cala Moli** is a secluded, sandy cove with a bar or two and some up-market villas in the hills above. **Cala Vedella** has been much more developed, to the point where its hillside villas and apartments are disproportionate to the space and the facilities in the bay below.

San Antonio Abad, a great concrete colossus on the west coast with an almost unlimited range of activities and nightlife, suffers from the considerable disadvantage of possessing the worst beach of any major Mediterranean resort; small, dirty and polluted. Visitors have little option but to make the trek by ferry to nearby sandy coves, which have the best of the self-catering accommodation, almost entirely apartments. Under no circumstances, however, does this fall into the category of a quiet place for a holiday.

Formentera

Lying just south of Ibiza, Formentera offers some of the quietest and most attractive beaches in the Balearics, but little else. Its principal resort, **Es Pujols,** in the north of the island, would scarcely rate a passing glance if it were situated on Majorca. Most of the self-catering accommodation consists of unpretentious apartments, some of it in 'holiday villages' with a swimming-pool and restaurant complex. With few exceptions, the kitchen facilities in studio and one-bedroom apartments consist only of simple rings, requiring the occupants to eat full meals in restaurants. Only larger apartments have a proper kitchen.

Apartments and a few isolated villas are also available at or near **La Sabina,** the little ferry port; **Playa Mitjorn,** a long sandy beach on the south coast marred by underwater rocks; and **Cala Sahona,** a deep cove on the west coast, though with unpredictable currents.

On Formentera, even quite common goods can suddenly be in short supply because of a surge in demand during the peak season. Repairs to household equipment can also take much longer than usual. There is a general shortage of water, most of which is drawn from wells and tastes rather salty. Fortunately, the local red wine is cheap and drinkable, and far superior to any other produced in the Balearics.

Getting there

Most travel to the Balearic Islands is by direct air charter. The approximate flight times of the principal routes are as follows:

From	Majorca	Minorca	Ibiza
Aberdeen	3¼		
Belfast	3		
Birmingham	2½	2½	2½
Bristol	2¼	2¼	2½
Cardiff	2¼	2¼	2½
East Midlands	2½	2½	2½
Edinburgh	3		
Exeter	2¼		
Gatwick	2¼	2¼	2¼
Glasgow	3	2¾	3
Heathrow	2¼	2¼	2¼
Leeds	2¼		2¾
Luton	2¾	2¼	2¼
Manchester	2½	2½	2¾
Newcastle	2¾	2¾	3
Norwich	2½		
Southend	2½		
Stansted	2¼	2¼	2¼
Teesside	2¾		

Majorca's Son San Juan airport is seven miles east of Palma. Minorca's Mahon airport is three miles south-west of Mahon. Ibiza's Es Codola airport is 5½ miles south-west of Ibiza town. Formentera does not possess an airport. Travel is via Ibiza.

The crossing from Ibiza to Formentera, 11 miles, takes about 1¼ hours. When you add baggage handling at Ibiza airport, about an hour in summer; the transfer to the ferry, plus average waiting time of 40 minutes; and the transfer to your accommodation on Formentera, 20 minutes, the entire journey may well take 3¼ hours. Add, say, a 2½-hour flight from the UK, and reaching Formentera can be the best part of a six-hour journey.

Ferries are available from the Spanish mainland to each of the three large islands. On Majorca, Palma is eight hours from Barcelona and nine hours from Valencia. On Minorca, Mahon is nine hours from Barcelona and sixteen hours from Valencia. On Ibiza, Ibiza town is six hours from Valencia and nine and a half hours from Barcelona.

Local transport

Apart from the ferry linking Ibiza to Formentera (see above), there are regular sailings between Majorca and Minorca (seven hours) and between Majorca and Ibiza (four and a half hours). There is no direct ferry service between Minorca and Ibiza.

Minorca Car hire is essential to make the most of a stay on Minorca, whose best beaches are not accessible by public transport. Mahon is the centre of an unreliable bus service. Smaller resorts have only a single return service daily, and many more remote places have no service at all. Cala Santa Galdana has particularly poor bus links considering its reputation as a resort.

Majorca Bus services are excellent along the coast road from Palma to the principal resorts, running until late at night. Services to the rest of the island are also reliable and cheap.

Alone of the Balearic Islands, Majorca also possesses a railway. The two rail routes, one to Arta in the north-east, the other to Soller in the north-west, are a scenic rather than a fast means of transport.

Taxis are plentiful and not expensive. However, in peak season drivers tend to overlook their meters. Agree on the fare in advance wherever possible.

Ibiza Bus services are frequent and cheap, but cannot cope with the influx in summer; expect them to be packed and suffocatingly hot after midday.

Almost all bus services come to an end by 9 p.m., which is a signal for taxis, modestly priced during the day, to acquire mysterious surcharges – if you can find one empty at all.

Visitors with hire car in Ibiza can often make use of a separate hire car on Formentera (see below).

Formentera Formentera has severe limitations in every aspect of transport. The island is only 10 miles long, with very few roads. Most bus services run only between the port and Es Pujols, and obtaining a taxi after midnight is almost impossible. A bicycle is the best means of transport, provided that you check both the tyres and the brakes.

The nightlife on Ibiza may also prove elusive, as the last ferry back to Formentera leaves at 8 p.m. Visitors staying on Formentera but wishing to visit Ibiza for a few days can leave their hire car at the departing ferry station and pick up another hire car on arrival. The scheme works in reverse for visitors staying on Ibiza who wish to see Formentera.

SPAIN

Weather
Minorca

Averages	Jan	Feb	Mar	Apr	May	Jun
Temperature	57	59	62	64	70	77
Sun hours	5	6	6	7	9	10
Rainy days	7	6	6	5	4	3
Sea temp.	56	57	57	61	66	70

Averages	Jul	Aug	Sep	Oct	Nov	Dec
Temperature	83	83	79	72	64	59
Sun hours	12	10	7	5	5	4
Rainy days	2	2	4	8	8	8
Sea temp.	75	78	73	68	65	60

Minorca receives more rain than Majorca but has similar temperatures during the summer. Only January is an unattractive month for a mid-winter holiday.

Majorca

Averages	Jan	Feb	Mar	Apr	May	Jun
Temperatures	57	59	62	66	72	79
Sun hours	5	6	6	8	9	11
Rainy days	6	5	5	4	3	2
Sea temp.	56	57	57	61	67	71

Averages	Jul	Aug	Sep	Oct	Nov	Dec
Temperature	84	84	77	74	64	59
Sun hours	11	10	8	6	5	4
Rainy days	1	2	4	7	7	7
Sea temp.	76	80	73	68	65	61

The south of Majorca has the driest weather: less than 16 inches of rain in a whole year. The north is much wetter, with an average rainfall of 32 inches.

Ibiza

Averages	Jan	Feb	Mar	Apr	May	Jun
Temperature	58	58	62	66	73	80
Sun hours	5	6	7	7	10	10
Rainy days	8	6	8	6	5	3
Sea temp.	56	57	57	61	67	71

Averages	Jul	Aug	Sep	Oct	Nov	Dec
Temperature	84	86	81	74	65	61
Sun hours	11	11	8	6	5	5
Rainy days	1	3	5	9	9	9
Sea temp.	76	80	73	68	65	61

Ibiza receives most of its rainfall – less than 16 inches annually – in the south and west of the island. Damp days consist of occasional showers rather than a continuous downpour. The temperature is extremely hot in summer and remains mild even in the middle of winter.

Formentera

Averages	Jan	Feb	Mar	Apr	May	Jun
Temperature	57	58	61	65	72	78
Sun hours	5	6	7	7	10	10
Rainy days	8	6	8	6	5	3
Sea temp.	56	57	57	62	68	72

Averages	Jul	Aug	Sep	Oct	Nov	Dec
Temperature	82	84	80	73	63	60
Sun hours	11	11	8	6	5	5
Rainy days	1	3	5	8	9	9
Sea temp.	77	80	74	68	66	62

Surprisingly, Formentera is slightly cooler than Ibiza, but the sea temperature is a degree or two higher for most of the year.

The Costas

The Spanish tourist industry was planned, if it were ever planned at all, on the basis of an ever-expanding and largely indiscriminate market. But there are strong indications that the 54 million foreign holiday-makers, more than 7 million of them British, who visited Spain in 1988 represent the country's peak of tourism. Many holiday-makers are no longer prepared to stay in accommodation inferior to their own homes. Many now recognise the mediocre fast-food restaurants for what they are. Many are taking seriously reports of sea and beach pollution.

Good news though this may be for the cause of change, it does not help the tourist searching the brochures for a low-cost self-catering holiday outside the concrete jungle of the Costas. Every British visitors who turns his back on a hotel package tour to, say, Salou – and there are a great many – is a potential competitor for more sophisticated and agreeable self-catering accommodation elsewhere on the coast. Better quality and higher prices reflect both demand and Spain's increasing determination to spend more on the local infrastructure. Nor are these higher prices offset by cheaper food, for, while restaurants still represent good value, supermarket shopping in Spain is conspicuously more expensive than it is in the UK.

The shift in priorities also makes independent self-catering holidays in mainland Spain more difficult to organise. Because of consolidation (industry-speak for cancellations arising from a downturn in business), tourists booked on one flight may find themselves travelling on a different day from the one originally confirmed, and arriving at a different airport – and even departing from a different airport in the UK. Independent travellers can still achieve low last-minute fares but, lacking the purchasing power of a major tour operator, they are also the most vulnerable to last-minute changes. In the peak season they can also no longer rely on organising for themselves apartment accommodation in the larger resorts on the spot. Self-catering flats are often fully booked in July and August when hotel holidays remain in plentiful supply.

Even when self-catering apartments are available on the spot at short notice, you may discover the exact standard of accommodation the hard way, as many owners avoid having their apartments officially classified. Where you come across such an apartment, it is safe to assume the worst.

Most villas on the Costas are not offered as part of a package tour. The best are often in villages nestling in the hills behind the coast, for which a car is essential. They are usually booked direct from newspaper or magazine advertisements placed by owners or agents. In many cases you will be given a contact number in the UK and can take advantage of the owner's detailed knowledge of the property and the district.

However, the usual caveats still apply. If you can pay at least the deposit and preferably the balance by credit card, you have some measure of protection should the accommodation not be as described. Ask for written details of the property and a written guarantee that it is yours exclusively for the period you have reserved. If you intend to book a night flight, check carefully that the accommodation is available for the night when you are actually travelling. If information sent to you does not provide an answer to points which are essential for the full enjoyment of your holiday, discuss them with the owner or agent. It may be unrealistic to expect them to put the answers in writing, so do so on their behalf, and send them by recorded delivery. In that way, if the owners or agents fail to contradict points which you have made clear are an essential precondition of your holiday reservation, you would have evidence for a subsequent claim for compensation.

Many resorts are served by more than one airport, and the transfer times vary sharply. Individual times have been included below for each of the major resort areas.

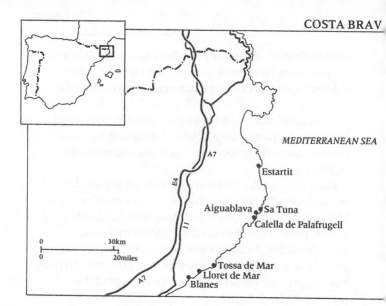

The Costa Brava

On the Costa Brava, the closest to the UK and also the cheapest, most of the resorts are brash and ugly, much of their accommodation built of crumbling concrete. But there are exceptions. One of them is **Calella de Palafrugell** (nearest airport Gerona, 1½ hours, but can be reached by way of Barcelona, 2½ hours). On no account mistake it for Calella de la Costa (see below), a disagreeable resort on the Costa Dorada but, confusingly, also served by Gerona and Barcelona airports. Calella de Palafrugell remains a small and friendly fishing village even though its steep and narrow cobbled streets are now full of bars, boutiques and cafés. It has a series of small sandy beaches in separate coves around the bay. The self-catering accommodation consists of villa, bungalow and low-level apartment developments among pine trees behind the village. The quality varies sharply, and though some complexes have direct access to the sea this is only by way of a formidable number of steps. Further north, a number of villas are available among the pine forests close to the villages of **Sa Tuna** and **Aiguablava,** within easy reach of some attractive tiny coves.

Also worth considering is **Tossa de Mar** (1 hour from Gerona, 2 hours from Barcelona or Reus), by far the most sophisticated of the large resorts. Skirted by the busy coast road, its development has been restricted by the hills surrounding three sides of the town and by medieval fortifications on the fourth. But the main beach, very safe, consisting of coarse sand, is still unable to cope in midsummer with the daily influx of coach-trippers, who also swamp the bars and shops of the old quarter. Fortunately, at night Tossa is much more serene, with many pleasant bars and restaurants. Its self-catering accommodation consists of apart-hotels and apartments, many a long climb from the beach; and at San Eloy, a chalet complex outside the resort, due for redevelopment.

Neighbouring **Lloret de Mar** (¾ hour from Gerona, 2¾ hours from Barcelona or Reus) is the liveliest resort on the Costa Brava, with a nightlife that leaves even the most determined teenagers fit to drop at dawn. Loret caters for what it considers to be British tastes: bacon, egg and sausage are offered almost 24 hours a day, while Wimpy and McDonald's have set up business in competition with dozens of snack bars and pizzerias whose fare is advertised by blaring music. Lloret's principal beach is of tiny pebbles. Many of its apartments lie a long way back from the shore and require a steep walk uphill.

Lloret is also the source of nightlife for **Blanes,** four miles to the south. Blanes (45 minutes from Gerona, 1½ hours from Barcelona or Reus) has an agreeable promenade, an interesting harbour with a marina, and some atmospheric narrow streets in the old quarter. The beach of fine pebbles slopes sharply at some points, so small children are not entirely secure. Many of the self-catering apartments are low-priced but poorly maintained.

Estartit, a family resort 27 miles east of Gerona (1¼ hours, Barcelona and Reus 2½ hours) with a strong emphasis on self-catering, has no through traffic and little nightlife. Its beach is long, flat and sandy, particularly safe for children, although there are occasional days of strong winds and big waves.

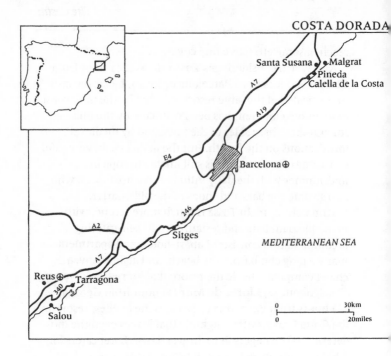

The Costa Dorada

Where the Costa Brava ends, the Costa Dorada begins.
Much of the coast (which has budget self-catering
accommodation) is marred by a main railway line,
polluted beaches and the urban sprawl of two cities,
Tarragona and Barcelona. Only **Sitges** (¾ hour from
Barcelona) escapes these huge disadvantages. It does have
a prominent railway, but its route runs well away from the
sea. As a consequence, the sandy beach, fringed by palm
trees and a gleaming promenade, is particularly attractive.
The beach narrows further west, where up-market villas
have been built, but the original coarse shingle has been
submerged in tons of Saharan sand imported from
Morocco. Unfortunately, at weekends the peace is ruined
when Spanish day-trippers turn up from Barcelona, an
hour away on the train.

At **Calella de la Costa** (1 hour from Gerona, 1½ hours

from Barcelona), the railway line runs between the unappealing apartment blocks and the beach, restricting access to a number of tunnels. The wire fence erected along its complete length has been penetrated in places by visitors bent on finding a short cut. The beach, much of it shingle, shelves steeply into the sea. The one redeeming factor for some visitors will be the hectic nightlife.

At **Malgrat** (45 minutes from Gerona, 1½ hours from Barcelona) the railway line is almost entirely unprotected, so the temptation to cross it is overwhelming. The beach, another mixture of sand and shingle, shelves just as steeply and its breakwater is an added danger. **Pineda** (1 hour from Gerona or Barcelona) would be an agreeable little town but for the railway barring the way to the sea. The beach is largely shingle and drops away sharply. At **Santa Susana** nothing has been done to reduce the effects of the inevitable sea-front railway line, which is almost entirely unprotected. The major resort of **Salou** (from Reus ½ hour, Barcelona 1¾ hours, Gerona 2½ hours) has no problems from its railway line and offers extensive self-catering apartments close to a fine beach, although the town has been blighted in the past by serious sea pollution from sewage.

The Costa Blanca

Perhaps the most attractive resort on the Costa Blanca, the central stretch of Spain's Mediterranean coastline, is **Puerto de Mazarron** (2 hours from Alicante), a small town specialising in self-catering. Situated on the southern edge of the Costa Blanca, beyond the famous city of Cartagena, it has pleasant beaches of fine sand, in a huge sheltered bay. Some of the more affluent Spaniards take their holidays here.

La Manga (1¾ hours from Alicante), located on a narrow promontory, has been transformed by the creation of a huge sports and leisure centre. Standing beside two 18-hole championship golf courses, it has an agreeable apartment village, backed by several swimming-pools. Its

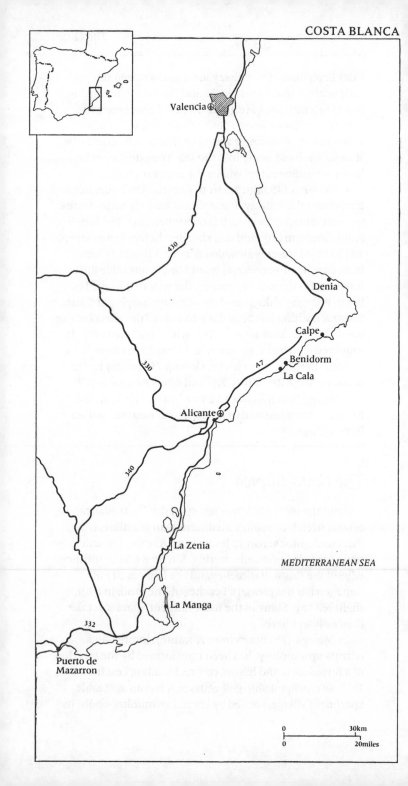

Valencia⊕

430

Denia

330

Calpe

A7

Benidorm

La Cala

Alicante⊕

340

La Zenia

MEDITERRANEAN SEA

La Manga

332

Puerto de
Mazarron

| 0 | | 30km |
| 0 | | 20miles |

other facilities include tennis, watersports, riding, squash, bowls and a health club. Children have their own entertainment, and babysitting is available. The beaches are white soft sand running into dunes. The sea can be rough – ideal for surfers but not for poor swimmers – but behind the resort lie the calm waters of an almost landlocked gulf.

North of La Manga, **La Zenia** (1½ hours from Alicante) is a small resort offering two agreeable and relatively quiet beaches. Despite considerable self-catering development, it has few amenities, apart from the golf course of Villamartin a few miles inland. Unfortunately, like other major courses in Spain, unless you book and pay for specific tee-off times well in advance, a wait of four or five hours to play is not unusual in summer.

The Costa Blanca is of course synonymous with **Benidorm** (1 hour from Alicante, 2½ hours from Valencia). The colossus of the Spanish tourist industry, Benidorm still attracts more British holiday-makers than any other overseas resort. Its sweeping panorama of concrete skyscrapers can accommodate 35,000 tourists, an entire city on vacation, packed into a pulsating pleasuredrome. Many of the apartments and apart-hotels are close to the principal beach, the Playa de Levante, gently shelving, soft white sand, ideal for children. To reach it you have to cross a busy dual carriageway.

Beyond Benidorm's harbour, rather more mediocre apartments face the Playa de Poniente, much narrower than the Levante beach and consequently more crowded; it is also appreciably noisier, because behind lies one of the main roads to Alicante and Valencia, with, despite a new bypass, fast and often heavy traffic.

At its southern end, Poniente widens out into the attractive suburb of **La Cala,** which has a series of quite luxurious villas and some well-appointed apartments. La Cala offers the best beach facilities in the resort – which has the disadvantage that other holiday-makers stake their claim early in the morning, using the shuttle buses that run from one end of Benidorm to the other.

A mere 15 minutes from its airport, **Alicante** lacks both

charm and character. Its large sandy beach is swamped by visitors in summer, and even more come simply on a day-trip to the shops. **Calpe** (1½ hours from Alicante, 2½ hours from Valencia) stands on a distinctive volcanic rock, which divides the beach, one side narrow and packed in summer, the other much wider and with space to spare, though interspersed with rocks and pebbles. Many of the self-catering bungalows, apartments and apart-hotels are located just below Calpe's extremely steep main shopping street, a stiff climb for young children and the elderly. There is a villa development just north of the town. **Denia** (2 hours from Alicante or Valencia) is largely a shopping centre for various self-catering complexes: villas, apartments and bungalows, on each side of the resort. Denia's beach of fine soft sand slopes gently into the sea, and is ideal for children.

The Costa de Almeria

At the eastern end of Spain's southern coast is the Costa de Almeria, taking its name from the prosperous provincial capital. Almeria has charter flights direct from the UK, a climate so dry that it makes the Costa del Sol seem positively damp, and one attractive self-catering resort close to the remarkable hilltop village of **Mojacar.** Visible for many miles, its white buildings on stepped hillsides shimmering in the sun, Mojacar clings determinedly to its Moorish past. The self-catering developments are outside the village. The best, close to the beach, consists of terraced town houses with two bedrooms and a well-equipped kitchen with a proper oven and a washing machine. Another apartment complex, on two and three floors in rather over-indulgent Moorish style, is further from the sea but has a huge swimming-pool. This is just as well, because other than being close to the nearby big hotels, the sandy beach is rough, untidy and quite unappealing. A series of high quality individual

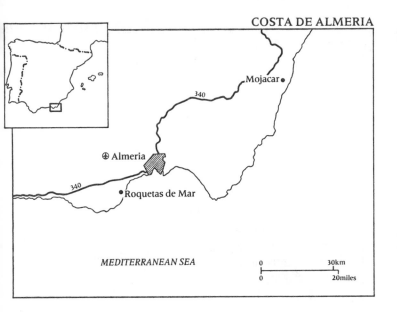

villas, many with private swimming-pools, has been built in the surrounding hills.

There is much less to recommend **Roquetas de Mar,** constructed on windswept salt-flats 12 miles south of Almeria (1 hour). Its connection with the original down-trodden village a mile away seems purely accidental. Modern Roquetas is centred on a single main street lined with hotels and largely nondescript apartments, although there are a few newer and well-furnished flats available on the sea-front. The beach of coarse sand shelves sharply into the sea and is not safe for small children.

187

The Costa del Sol

Cloudless summer skies, warm tranquil seas and vivid
mountain scenery sustain tourism to the Costa del Sol
when the other Costas look gloomily at a declining
number of visitors. This is especially true at the luxury end
of the market, as the demand for secluded, high quality
houses with exceptional furnishings and private
swimming-pools remains as high as ever. While some of
the big resorts, notably Fuengirola, Marbella and
Torremolinos, have made epic architectural blunders, their
nightlife remains relentless and exciting, and at each of
them apartments are readily available at budget to much
higher prices.

For more sophisticated visitors, **Nerja,** east of Malaga
(1½ hours), now seems to have acquired a reputation as
the leading self-catering resort. A small Moorish town with
shaded patios and narrow streets, it was unable to

accommodate major development, which has largely occurred in the hills behind. In all, three major complexes exist, each with outstanding coastal views. The accommodation covers the full range of studios, apartments, maisonettes and villas, supported by what amounts almost to a small town of bars, restaurants, swimming-pools and shops. Some of the flats are built into the hillside and have steep access steps; the climb from the nearest beach is quite demanding, too. Nerja also has an exceptionally high number of individual villas, many British owned and rented direct. The town is inundated with visitors in summer but remains comparatively subdued in comparison to the resorts east of Malaga.

Time has no meaning in **Torremolinos,** where many holiday-makers reach their beds after dawn. The noise is so enormous that it is often difficult to distinguish between the dozen different languages spoken around the outdoor tables. High-rise hotels, apart-hotels and budget apartments have been constructed so close to one another that many of the rooms exist in a zone of perpetual twilight. The beach of rather grubby grey sand runs imperceptibly into **Benalmadena Costa,** which has a rather more down-market nightlife, if such a concept seems possible.

As Benalmadena also possesses some of the better quality apartments, the visitor has the invidious choice between agreeable accommodation and disagreeable surroundings. Fortunately, high quality villas, many with private swimming-pools, are available in the foothills behind the town. Some smart apartments have also been built at **Arroyo de la Miel,** a village with superior and cheaper restaurants than Benalmadena itself.

Just under 30 miles from Torremolinos, **Marbella** (1 hour from Malaga) attracts many holiday-makers who imagine that they will be cheek by jowl with the jet-set. In reality the rich and famous stay on yachts and eat in restaurants well beyond the average tourist's pocket. Marbella proper leads on to a cramped beach of imported sand. The better beaches, and the best villas and apartments, are anything up to ten miles outside the town.

189

Only one quality complex is near Marbella itself, a 'pueblo'-style village on the residential slopes behind the town centre. Each villa or apartment has a washing machine and that comparative rarity in self-catering, a dishwasher. As for the lines of millionaires' yachts, they lie four miles away in the marina of **Puerto Banus,** whose boutiques and restaurants charge prices apparently based on the income of the owners, not the passers-by.

Puerto Banus, a modern interpretation of what a medieval Andalucian fishing village might have looked like (but never did), runs into **Nueva Andalucia,** well back from the sea, and with the best of the self-catering accommodation apart from luxury attached villas. Take, for example, a semicircle of Moorish-style town houses and apartments around a central pool, furnished in the grand manner with designer kitchens complete with washing machine and that elusive dishwasher.

Several far-from-luxurious high-rise apartments can be found at or near **Fuengirola** (½ hour from Malaga). The occupants, mainly on a budget holiday, often simply do not have the resources for an extravagant or costly meal out. This may explain why Fuengirola, a sprawling resort like Torremolinos, has no focal-point. The beach, though slightly grey, is its biggest asset – four miles of sand, interrupted by a small fishing harbour, and backed by many small restaurants and a promenade. The busy coast road is a major problem for families, as in almost every case they have to cross it to reach the sea. The most promising development of villas and apartments, three miles west of the town, has a tunnel under the road to the nearest beach which at this point consists largely of rocks.

Estepona (1½ hours from Malaga) remains ripe for redevelopment but has major disadvantages as a resort: it is located on the busy main coast road and overlooks a narrow beach of drab, dark sand. This is perhaps why many package tours attributed to Estepona refer in fact to apartments that may be as close, or closer, to Marbella to the east or Algeciras to the west. **Benamara**, nine miles towards Marbella, is a group of multiple villa and apartment complexes that have helped to elevate the location to the status of resort. The best are on the beach side of the main road, with their own swimming-pools and gardens.

Getting there

Most travel to the Spanish Costas is by direct air charter. The approximate flight times of the principal routes are as follows:

From	Barcelona Reus Gerona	Alicante Valencia	Almeria Malaga
Belfast	2¾		3¼
Birmingham	2¼	2¾	2¾
Bristol	2¼	2½	2½
Cardiff	2¼	2½	2½
East Midlands	2¼	2¾	2¾
Edinburgh	2¾	3	
Gatwick	2	2¼	2¾
Glasgow	2¾	3	3¼
Heathrow	2	2½	2¾
Leeds	2½	3	
Luton	2	2¼	2¾
Manchester	2½	2¾	3
Newcastle	2½	2¾	3¼
Stansted	2¼		
Teesside			3¼

By car the Costa Brava (a journey of at least 18 hours) is just under 800 miles via Cherbourg, around 860 miles via the shortest Channel crossings, and about 450 miles by way of the Plymouth–Santander ferry. By the same routes the Costa del Sol (at least 32 hours) is about 1170, 1340 and 600 miles respectively.

By coach the resorts on the Costa Brava and Costa Dorada can be reached between 24 and 28 hours.

By train from London via Calais the Spanish Mediterranean border can be reached in under 24 hours; there are connections at Port-Bou to Barcelona and Valencia.

Local transport

Costa Brava Bus services are cheap, comfortable and fast on the main coast route, less reliable and slower inland. In summer buses can be extremely crowded, but on most routes a seat can be booked in advance. A circular shuttle bus service operates in the main resorts, such as Lloret de Mar, linking the beaches and the principal self-catering areas. At the peak of the season long, disorderly queues build up at bus stops.

Costa Dorada For holiday-makers without a car, the local bus service is of particular importance in view of the distance between villas and the centre of large towns, such as Tarragona and Salou. On the main coast road, buses run at 30-minute intervals until late at night in summer. The main railway, which blights the resorts of Calella de la Costa, Malgrat, Pineda and Santa Susana, is also a quick means of access (about an hour) to Barcelona, with ten trains in each direction daily during the summer.

Costa Blanca Long-distance buses operate a frequent service from Barcelona to Alicante (about ten hours) and other Costa Blanca destinations; advance booking is essential during the summer. In Benidorm buses are extremely simple to use because there are only four interlocking services, each with a uniform fare. A shuttle bus service operates along the sea-front.

Costa de Almeria Mojacar is distinguished by its complete absence of public transport. More unscrupulous independent visitors tend to merge with the package holiday-makers to take advantage of their free shuttle bus service connecting the Hotel Indalo, the Puebla Indalo and the Hotel Moresco, which in summer operates every half-hour between 10 a.m. and midnight. Long queues are common.

Costa del Sol With so many villas and apartments located outside the main resorts, for the visitor without a car bus services take on a particular importance. Fortunately they are both cheap and extremely frequent. More than 30 buses a day link Marbella to Malaga and almost as many Fuengirola to Torremolinos, despite the equally frequent electric railway.

Spanish Motorail, Auto-Expreso, will transport your car from Madrid to Malaga, linking with the French Motorail service between Madrid and Paris, although services leave from different Madrid stations.

Weather
The Costa Brava

Averages	Jan	Feb	Mar	Apr	May	Jun
Temperature	56	57	61	64	70	77
Sun hours	5	5	6	8	8	10
Rainy days	3	4	5	4	5	4
Sea temp.	55	55	55	57	61	68

Averages	Jul	Aug	Sep	Oct	Nov	Dec
Temperature	82	82	77	70	61	57
Sun hours	10	10	8	6	4	4
Rainy days	2	4	5	7	4	5
Sea temp.	72	73	72	68	61	57

The Costa Brava can be extremely hot in high season, with many days of sustained sunshine. The temperature is at its most comfortable in May and October, but October can be a wet month. The winters are far from warm.

The Costa Dorada

Averages	Jan	Feb	Mar	Apr	May	Jun
Temperature	56	57	61	65	71	77
Sun hours	5	5	6	8	8	10
Rainy days	3	3	5	5	5	4
Sea temp.	53	53	54	55	59	66

Averages	Jul	Aug	Sep	Oct	Nov	Dec
Temperature	82	82	77	71	61	57
Sun hours	10	10	8	6	4	4
Rainy days	2	4	5	6	4	5
Sea temp.	71	71	70	66	60	55

The Costa Dorada is hot in June, July, August and September but not entirely free from rain. July is the driest month, but curiously the next driest are January and February, though they are rather cold. October is the wettest month, but much drier than the Costa Brava.

The Costa Blanca

Averages	Jan	Feb	Mar	Apr	May	Jun
Temperature	61	62	66	70	75	82
Sun hours	6	6	6	8	10	10
Rainy days	4	4	4	5	4	2
Sea temp.	57	57	58	61	62	69

Averages	Jul	Aug	Sep	Oct	Nov	Dec
Temperature	88	88	84	77	68	62
Sun hours	12	10	8	7	6	4
Rainy days	1	1	4	5	4	4
Sea temp.	70	74	69	64	62	57

The Costa Blanca is extremely hot and dry during July and August, with sustained sunshine. May and October have a more pleasant temperature, but the risk of rain is considerably greater. The temperature remains high by UK standards from late March to late November, although the winter nights are cold.

The Costa de Almeria

Averages	Jan	Feb	Mar	Apr	May	Jun
Temperature	62	62	65	71	77	84
Sun hours	6	6	7	8	10	12
Rainy days	3	2	1	0	0	0
Sea temp.	59	58	59	61	63	70

Averages	Jul	Aug	Sep	Oct	Nov	Dec
Temperature	88	89	84	76	67	64
Sun hours	12	12	10	8	6	6
Rainy days	0	0	1	2	2	3
Sea temp.	73	75	71	65	63	68

The Costa de Almeria has a mild climate similar to the Costa del Sol's, although evenings tend to be significantly cooler out of season. Even in winter there is very little rain – less than eight inches on average in a year – making this one of the driest regions in Europe.

The Costa del Sol

Averages	Jan	Feb	Mar	Apr	May	Jun
Temperature	62	62	65	70	76	83
Sun hours	6	6	6	8	10	11
Rainy days	6	5	6	5	2	0
Sea temp.	59	58	59	61	63	70

Averages	Jul	Aug	Sep	Oct	Nov	Dec
Temperature	87	88	84	76	67	64
Sun hours	12	11	9	7	6	5
Rainy days	0	0	2	6	5	5
Sea temp.	70	75	70	65	63	58

The Costa del Sol has practically no rain in summer, long hours of sunshine, and extremely high temperatures. In April, May and October and early November it is still warmer than many Mediterranean resorts become in midsummer. The winter temperature is warm and sunny, but with an appreciable risk of rain.

Making the booking

A self-catering holiday may prove to be both a great success and superb value for money – or it can be hugely overpriced and come perilously close to disaster.

There is no easy way for the holiday-maker to find the ideal property at the ideal price. Even this guide to self-catering accommodation cannot possibly identify individual properties – be they cottages or castles, villas or bungalows, apartments or studios – owned and let on a personal basis by their owners.

The guide also cannot recommend specific accommodation offered by tour operators, mainly because of the sheer numbers involved with hundreds of thousands of properties available. The market is extremely erratic, too, with owners frequently switching allegiance from one holiday company to another, or taking their property off the rental market, or changing its availability from season to season. Very few properties are actually owned by the company or companies offering them for rent, making control over their availability and upkeep extremely difficult. Another factor is the lack of proper supervision of the market, in which owners, agents, tour operators and local representatives are not required to satisfy a Code of Conduct applying specifically to self-catering.

The list in this guide of companies and operators specialising in self-catering in each country should therefore be regarded as simply that. The list is not a guarantee of quality, or of consistency, or of value – even reputable companies sometimes market unsatisfactory properties – but is a list of organisations that offer self-catering accommodation in the appropriate country.

There are two key questions that can help to distinguish between the organisations offering self-catering. They are:

• Does the organiser contract direct with the owner of each property, as distinct from any agents or intermediaries?

• Does the organisation have a representative in the immediate vicinity fluent in the local language and responsible for sorting out any problems that may occur?

Put these questions before you book. A positive answer to both makes it more likely that the property is competitively priced and looked after carefully on the spot. Refer to the answers in writing when booking, so that if the information proves to be misleading you have a record of what was said.

Travel agents, ostensibly a good source of advice, in practice rarely play a significant role in self-catering holiday arrangements. They are not geared to self-catering holiday enquiries outside a few large companies. Some travel agents also allow their staff to accept incentives from major tour operators to sell their products, irrespective of their suitability, in preference to others on the market.

Direct sales are common in this market. Many reputable self-catering organisations decline to give commission to travel agents. Even when a self-catering holiday is booked with a large company through a travel agent, the company may still take many more reservations direct by telephone.

The majority of self-catering holiday-makers do not book through travel agents and often have to make their own judgement on the security of their holiday. Specialists in self-catering are no safer than other companies in what has become a volatile travel industry.

Bookings are secure when made with a company that is a tour-operator member of the Association of British Travel Agents (ABTA). ABTA tour-operator members often sell both direct and through a travel agent, but the agent also has to be an ABTA member. Anyone who buys a holiday direct with an ABTA operator or through an ABTA travel agent is sure of a refund or being able to finish his holiday if the tour operator goes bust. Should the ABTA agent go out of business while still holding his money, the holiday-maker's holiday would still be guaranteed or, at worst, he would be given his money back. You can check whether a tour operator or a travel agent is a current member of ABTA by telephoning the Association of British Travel Agents on 071-637 2444 between 9 and 5.30, Monday to Friday.

Non-ABTA tour operators are equally secure provided that they are offering recognised inclusive tour arrangements – flight, plus transfers, plus self-catering accommodation. These operators have to be bonded together under the terms of the company's Air Tours Operator's Licence (ATOL), guaranteeing that should a company cease trading any of its clients already abroad would be able to complete their holiday, and any clients still to travel would receive a full refund. Always check whether a company claiming to offer inclusive arrangements possesses its own ATOL, or the circumstances in which it is making use of an ATOL owned by another tour company. You can do this by asking for its ATOL number, and checking who actually owns the particular licence with the Civil Aviation Authority (telephone 071-379 7311) between 8.30 and 5.40, Monday to Friday.

Some smaller self-catering operators are members of the Association of Independent Tour Operators (AITO), which runs its own bonding scheme. Ferry companies that also offer self-catering holidays are part of the Passenger Shipping Association (PSA), which has its own bonding arrangements. But a number of smaller self-catering organisations do not operate inclusive arrangements involving charter flights or ferry bookings and are not part of these schemes. This is where the prospective holiday-maker is most vulnerable.

The best advice is to pay at least the deposit for self-catering accommodation from such a company only using a credit card (Access or Visa; American Express and Diner's Club are not credit but charge cards, as you are expected to meet their bill in full each month). Should that company cease trading, then you would be able to recover your money in full from the credit card company. Any organisation without credit card facilities should be treated with caution.

Most self-catering accommodation is booked from brochures. Although the standard of accuracy and candour in brochures has markedly improved, some companies remain economical with the truth. It remains essential to talk to a representative of the company about the specific property you intend to rent, and, in making the booking, to write to the company making detailed references to the amenities on which you are basing your decision. If the information given to you were to prove subsequently to have been misleading, only then would you have a real chance of claiming compensation.

People who book properties advertised by owners or their representatives in newspapers and magazines have no protection, except in those very rare circumstances when payment by credit card is possible. Asking the owner to put you in touch with someone else who booked the property the previous year can provide an encouraging reassurance. Legal remedy against owners who live in the UK is much easier to achieve than against owners resident abroad.

Holidays by air

Most self-catering holidays taken in Greece, Portugal or Spain, a substantial number in Italy and a significant number in France involve the use of air transport. With the exception of France, which places difficulties in the way of a mass charter market, the overwhelming majority of journeys are by cheap charter flight, either independently or as part of an inclusive self-catering holiday.

Charter flights to the leading self-catering holiday destinations can vary enormously in terms of convenience. Aircraft remain potentially profitable only when actually in the air, so multiple turnarounds in each 24-hour period are commonplace. For a busy aircraft on short-haul routes, at least one departure in each direction must take off or land (or possibly both) at night. Quite apart from any loss of sleep they may suffer, passengers may find that this has considerable knock-on effects on the price of their trip.

For example, a departure from a UK airport before 7 a.m. more or less obliges all passengers living some distance away, unless they choose to camp out at the terminal, to book into a hotel near the airport, thereby adding to their costs. Should they then arrive at their destination at around breakfast time, their apartments or villas may well not be vacated by departing guests until noon, forcing the new arrivals to wait around for several hours, tired and dishevelled. When, a fortnight later, it is time to leave, they could find the departure time also works to their disadvantage. Should their flight leave for home at, say, 1 or 2 a.m., they may be required to vacate their villa or apartment anything up to ten hours before they need to leave for the airport. On many flights their arrival time could compel them to spend another half-night in an airport hotel back in the UK, pushing up their costs still further.

When selecting a flight, satisfy yourself that all the disagreeable details have been disclosed by asking the following questions:

● Does the price include airport taxes? Even if the UK tax is quoted as an extra, you may still have to pay a further tax at the destination airport for the return leg. If the price is tax-exclusive, how much extra will you have to pay?

● Does the price include a weekend surcharge, if there is one? Does the operator reserve the right to impose a fuel-cost surcharge? If so, is there a limit on the increase, and is there a final date after which it will not be charged? If the final price is too high, do you have the right to cancel?

● Is the flight protected in any way under an Air Tour Operator's Licence? If so, what is the number?

● What type of aircraft will be used? Is it the same type in both directions?

● Is your hold luggage included in the price of the ticket (a very few airlines charge extra) and what is your baggage allowance?

● Can your luggage be checked through to your final destination if your flight involves touching down somewhere to refuel or for passengers to change planes?

● What is the takeoff time, duration and arrival time of each flight in each direction?

● What meals will be served? Are they hot or cold, and are they included in the price of the ticket (they are excluded on a few airlines)?

- What is the transfer time between your destination airport and your accommodation, and is the cost of the transfer included in the price?

- Whom do you contact to check that your return flight is operating to schedule?

The biggest hassle on your holiday may occur long before you travel. If the charter flight on which you are booked, or the inclusive tour of which the charter flight is an intrinsic part, does not sell well, the tour operator may decide to exercise an option it has with the carrier – to cancel the flight . . . or rather, as many flights are shared between operators, to pull out of its commitment to buy a certain number of seats at an agreed bulk rate on that flight, which may well continue to exist, with another operator taking up the newly available seat allocation. This procedure, known as 'consolidation', is the explanation behind something that perplexes and irritates many holiday-makers, who find that the flight on which they were told that they could no longer travel did in fact leave according to its original schedule.

Meanwhile, the tour operator, not always as quickly as it might, has informed its client or the client's travel agent that the flight arrangements have been changed. In the worst set of circumstances, the holiday-maker could find that:

- his departure airport had been altered, sometimes by hundreds of miles if he had originally planned to fly from a provincial airport,

- his day of departure had changed, sometimes reducing the length of his holiday, or

- the time of his flight had changed from day to night, perhaps forcing him to spend a night in a hotel near the UK airport prior to departure, or perhaps costing him a day or part of a day at his destination.

A holiday-maker can even find that his self-catering accommodation has been changed, possibly from one resort to another.

Many tour operators have what they call a trading charter, which gives the holiday-maker a choice when his holiday is, in the trade jargon, 'consolidated' in this way. He can accept the alterations and with them a reduction in the price to compensate for the inconvenience, usually calculated on a sliding scale according to the length of notice; he can opt to take a different holiday offered by the same tour operator, plus similar compensation; or he can cancel altogether, have all his money returned, and sometimes similar compensation as well.

Unfortunately, the offer to cancel is rarely an attractive one because finding an agreeable alternative for the same dates may be both difficult and more expensive. Likewise, holiday-makers may have set their hearts on a particular resort or property and not wish to go somewhere else.

The level of compensation offered initially is rarely sufficient to cover the costs of the changed arrangements, especially when they involve switching to another airport. Some holiday-makers have been successful in obtaining substantially higher payments from tour operators, particularly to compensate for long journeys to the changed airport, extra accommodation and meals. But this can be a long drawn-out process and might well not be settled before the holiday takes place.

Next to consolidation, surcharges are the cause of most complaints. Many companies in recent years have offered a no-surcharge guarantee subject only to 'governmental action', but the position can alter from summer to summer. Where surcharges can be imposed at the discretion of the tour operator, they may sometimes be limited to ten per cent of the cost of the holiday, above which the holiday-maker has the option to cancel. ABTA tour operators are now required to absorb surcharges of up to two per cent of the price of the holiday.

Most tour operators calculate the final cost of a holiday some 12 weeks before the final departure date, when the carrier will know his fuel price (calculated in US dollars) and will pass on any unexpected increases to the tour operator. Where its booking conditions permit, the tour operator will add any surcharge to its final account, which can include an element to cover the extra cost of any unsold seats on the flight.

The Code of Conduct of the Association of British Travel Agents lays down that the price increase must be 'for reasons beyond the control' of the tour operator, and anyone who asks must be provided with 'a reasonable written explanation of the reasons for the additional charge'. Holiday-makers who persist in asking tour operators for 'further and better particulars' of the reason for their surcharges have been known to have them reduced or even cancelled altogether. Although it is unusual for surcharges to be added after the final invoice has been paid, strictly speaking there is nothing to prevent a tour operator from doing so if its booking conditions do not prevent it: operators with little interest in repeat business have been known to collect surcharges at the airport departure gate.

Many hassles can be avoided by a following a simple check-list from the moment you book a flight. Answer the following questions.

On booking:

- Is your passport valid?

- Are you insured for the risk of cancellation?

Two weeks after booking, or sooner if your flight is due to leave within a fortnight:

- Has the cheque you gave as a deposit been cashed, or, better still, if you paid by credit card has the charge appeared on your statement?

- Has the airline, travel agent or tour operator acknowledged your booking and sent you an invoice confirming your flights (and self-catering accommodation) and indicating when the balance should be paid?

In the last week before you travel:

- Have you arranged foreign currency, traveller's cheques, a Eurocheque encashment card?

- Have you received your airline tickets and are the flights confirmed?

  In the last 24 hours:

- Have you telephoned the airline to confirm that you are listed on the flight?

- Are you certain of your departure airport and, where applicable, which terminal?

- Have you arranged your travel to the airport?

  Just before you leave home:

- Telephone the airport to establish whether the flight is likely to leave on time.

Holidays with a car

Mainland Spain remains the cheapest of the major Mediterranean countries in which to hire a car; prices are slightly higher in the islands. The costs increase successively in Portugal, Italy, France and Greece, and prices in Greece can be double those of Spain. Some self-catering packages include the price of a hire car, and fly-drive arrangements with substantial discounts on the car rental are available on scheduled flights.

The condition of hire cars does not improve significantly by using one of the major international companies: however, if the original vehicle breaks down, the availability of a replacement car does.

Beware misleadingly low quotations, especially from local firms, which may not be realised when the final price is presented. Personal accident insurance and a collision damage waiver are essential; not taking this cover is to invite complications later. A bail bond is vital in Spain (see page 208).

Most hire firms accept a blank, signed credit card voucher as a deposit. Try to return the car at the end of the holiday inside office hours, as disputing subsequently an incorrect bill entered on a pre-signed voucher can be extremely difficult.

UK rental companies may prove strangely unenthusiastic if you try to hire one of their cars – perhaps because you need a bigger car than the one you own – for the purpose of driving it on the wrong side of the road over several thousand miles. Most companies prefer you to hire two separate cars rather than to take a right-hand drive model to the Continent. This has two advantages: it saves the cost of transporting the car by ferry, and it provides you with the safest driving position for each part of your journey. But these advantages can be outweighed by the inconvenience of taking your luggage on the ferry in both directions.

If you do find a UK rental company willing to let you take a right-hand-drive model abroad, it still probably will not permit you to take the original registration document with you. As a photocopy is not acceptable, you need an International Registration Certificate for a Vehicle on Hire, obtainable from the AA or RAC (form V103). To complete it you need full details of the actual vehicle you are proposing to drive, including chassis and engine numbers.

If you are driving a hire car to Portugal, a special certificate is necessary, obtainable from the AA or RAC. It must be endorsed by the car rental company and stamped by the appropriate motoring organisation.

Documents

When taking your own car abroad, you may occasionally be asked to produce the vehicle registration document. If this is not available for some reason, you can obtain a Temporary Vehicle Certificate from any Local Vehicle Licensing Office by producing the current tax disc and your passport. Complete form V379, unless the car is brand new, in which case complete form V204.

A British driving licence is acceptable in each of the countries covered by this book, if you are aged 18 or over, although few overseas rental companies will hire out a car to anyone under 21. In Italy you are required to carry an Italian translation, obtainable by post from the AA or RAC, inside your licence. In Spain you must hold an International Driving Permit, also obtainable from the AA or RAC. Take along a passport-sized photograph of yourself, your current British licence, and complete a simple form. If you cannot produce your British licence, your entitlement to an IDP will be checked with the DVLC in Swansea by telephone before it is issued.

Insurance

Your UK car insurance policy gives you, when you take your own car abroad, the minimum insurance required by law in all EC countries, except Greece, where a 'Green Card' remains obligatory. This Green Card – the International Motor Insurance Card – is evidence of an extension to the UK policy to provide full insurance abroad. Obtainable from your motor insurance company, it is strongly recommended for all mainland European countries as well as Greece because the minimum cover can be very restrictive. Although under revision, at present this cover does not automatically include damage to a policy-holder's own car, and in some countries it does not cover death or injuries sustained by passengers. In Spain, even with a Green Card, a policy-holder involved in an accident could be arrested and his vehicle impounded unless he is also carrying a bail bond – a guarantee of a minimum sum of money acceptable to the authorities that your insurance company will post as bail should you be involved in a major accident.

Vehicle recovery insurance, offered by the AA, RAC and Europ Assistance, is equally vital. The policy covers the vehicle and its occupants, insuring against the cost of roadside assistance, towing and storage charges, air freighting spare parts; a hire car while your own is off the road undergoing repair; and the return of the car and the repatriation of its passengers to the UK if repairs cannot be completed in time for your return journey. Without insurance, recovering the vehicle and returning home at your own expense could cost many hundreds of pounds.

Vehicle requirements

When driving on the Continent, a UK-registered car must carry at the rear a GB nationality sticker or plate, white with black lettering, oval in shape, not less than 4½ inches high and 7 inches wide. The individual letters must be at least 3 inches high and 1 inch wide. You will also need a headlight conversion kit, obtainable from most garages, to change the direction of the headlamp beams to suit driving on the right. In France, if you normally wear spectacles for driving, you are required to carry a spare pair. In France, Italy and Spain you are expected to carry a set of replacement bulbs for side and brake lights. In Italy you are obliged to fit an exterior rear view mirror on the left-hand side of your right-hand-drive car. In Greece you must carry a first-aid kit and a fire extinguisher. A warning triangle is required everywhere on the Continent.

Problems

Motoring law on the Continent is different in some respects from that in the UK. In many countries the minimum permitted tyre tread depth may be as much as two millimetres, compared to one millimetre in the UK. Giving way to vehicles on the right remains a common, though not uniform, requirement. In Spain drivers who have held a licence for under a year must observe a 55 mph speed-limit. In France overtaking is forbidden within 100 metres of the brow of a hill. In Italy motorists must use their indicators when coming to a stop.

If you are involved in an accident in France, the police will produce an accident form called a *'constat'*, which must be completed in French and signed by all involved. Failure to do so will almost certainly result in your being arrested.

Substantial on-the-spot fines for minor offences, such as speeding or illegal parking, are commonplace throughout the Mediterranean resort areas. In most countries the police both issue the penalty and collect the fine. Payment in cash remains more or less obligatory.

Sharing

In many parts of the Continent, but particularly in France and Italy, very large properties are offered for rent, including medieval castles and genuine châteaux.

Few families on their own would have either the means or the inclination to take on a property with perhaps 20 rooms at their disposal. But by sharing with friends they can achieve a spectacular economy of scale.

The snag, of course, is that sharing can also lead to the end of a beautiful friendship. The key question to be faced long before everyone agrees on the choice of property and the bookings are finalised must be: do you really like the people concerned enough to spend every waking hour of the day with them for a fortnight or longer?

If you have a choice, choose people who never expect you to make a special effort for them, and whose lifestyle is similar to your own. Sharing a holiday with a childless couple who are happy only in gourmet restaurants that you cannot really afford, or whose only experience of your children is when they are safely tucked up in bed, could be a recipe for disaster.

Even if everyone concerned will fit into a single car, think twice before sharing the transport arrangements. The ability to escape from one another may become vitally important before the holiday is over. Separate cars also allow each of the parties concerned to take their own decision on excursions and detours.

If a single car is essential for reasons of economy, agree

on the route beforehand, including the number of miles you plan to travel each day, how long each person will be driving and where you intend to stay.

Any sharing arrangements should be placed on a professional footing from the start. Agree from the outset (and make a note of) the proportions that each couple or family will carry of any shared cost. Try to persuade all parties concerned that one person should be responsible for all the financial arrangements and the 'group' holiday paperwork, such as travel tickets or car insurance.

Another person should be given the task of checking the personal documentation of everyone travelling. If one of the party fails to renew a passport or overlooks personal insurance, the consequences could inconvenience everyone or even ruin the holiday.

However generous and well intentioned they are, people do become confused about the shared costs of a holiday, such as ferry bookings, Motorail, car insurance or accommodation deposits. The only certain method to avoid any bad feeling is to keep a proper set of accounts so that everyone can see what has been, and will be, spent.

Once the holiday is underway, the only conspicuously fair method to operate a sharing arrangement is to have a float of money into which each adult or couple contributes on the same pro-rata basis as the rent for the property. This float is then used to pay for all 'pooled' items, such as food, cleaning materials, electricity and, with a single car in use, petrol. Every item should be noted, removing any possibility of dispute.

If this seems unnecessarily pedantic, be warned that many groups of friends have set out on holiday together believing themselves to be above such petty disputes, only to vow later never to go abroad again under similar circumstances without organising the finances down to the last penny.

There is something to be said for adopting the same procedure for household chores, such as cooking, washing up, cleaning and shopping, so that no one's generosity is exploited.

Unless the children quarrel, families seem to get on

together better than couples. The late Russell Harty, once persuaded against his better judgement to join three couples in a shared villa in Provence, described his experience in a Sunday magazine article. According to Harty, the multiple sharing arrangements led to ludicrous levels of competition – even over who had swum the most lengths of the pool or achieved the highest gastronomic heights.

Tour operators

Nearly 250 companies, clubs, organisations and tour operators offer self-catering accommodation in one or more of the five Mediterranean countries featured in this book. They are listed alphabetically, together with their address, postcode and telephone number.

If they belong to ABTA or have their own ATOL, this is indicated, as is membership of AITO or PSA. Details of these bonding arrangements, which can change at short notice, are given on pages 197–8.

The regions in which each organisation offers self-catering are listed. Where a list refers to a country or countries instead of a region, it usually means that the particular organisation offers self-catering in a large number of different areas of that country.

The areas in which a company offers self-catering are liable to alteration at short notice. Companies may also offer additional self-catering in areas or countries not included in this book. Companies that offer self-catering only in other areas or countries, or in mobile homes, are not included.

This list should not be interpreted as a recommendation of individual companies or their products, or as a guarantee of their security. The self-catering holiday market is particularly volatile: companies regularly come and go, and the accommodation they offer can change from year to year. No distinction is made in the list between types of accommodation available.

The initial advice must be to ask for a brochure, which can usually be ordered by telephone on the number listed, often linked to a 24-hour answerphone. The brochure should include the company's ABTA number, where it is currently a member, and ATOL number, where it has one. It should also indicate whether payment may be made by credit card.

Where a company indicates that it is the 'agent for an ATOL holder' this may mean that only flights are bonded and that if payment is made in cash or by cheque a refund on the accommodation may not be guaranteed in the event of the rental company going bust.

Aer Lingus Holidays
56 High Street
Belfast BT1 2PU
Belfast (0232) 241110
ABTA, ATOL
Crete, The Algarve, The Estoril coast, Costa del Sol, Majorca

Agence France Holidays
23 Elizabeth Street
London SW1W 9RW
071-824 8910
Brittany, The Dordogne

Airlink Holidays
9 Wilton Road
London SW1V 1LL
071-828 7682
ABTA, ATOL
Corfu, Crete, Rhodes, The Algarve, Minorca

Airtours
Wavell House, Helmshore
Rossendale
Lancashire BB4 4NB
Rossendale (0706) 240011
ABTA, ATOL
The Algarve, Costa Blanca, Costa de Almeria, Majorca, Minorca, Ibiza

Albir Travel
Albir House
PO Box 292, Orpington
Kent BR6 8QG
Farnborough (0689) 50115
ATOL
Ibiza

Algarve Asset Management
Shirehill, Saffron Walden
Essex CB11 3AQ
Saffron Walden (0799) 26122
The Algarve

Algarve Select
The Red House
Kings Ride Court
Kings Ride, Ascot
Berkshire SL5 7JR
Ascot (0990) 28666
The Algarve

Allans Holidays
El Granero, Edenhall
Penrith
Cumbria CA11 8SX
Penrith (0768) 81536
Majorca

Allegro Holidays
15a Church Street, Reigate
Surrey RH2 OAA
Reigate (0737) 221323
ABTA, ATOL, AITO
Rhodes, Neapolitan Riviera,
The Algarve, Costa del Sol

Allez France
27 West Street
Storrington, Pulborough
West Sussex RH20 4DZ
Lancing (0903) 745319
ABTA
Provence and the Côte d'Azur,
Brittany, The Dordogne, Paris

Alternative Majorca
see Majorca Apartments and
Villas

Amathus
51 Tottenham Court Road
London W1P 0HS
071-636 9873
ABTA, ATOL
Corfu, Crete

Andrews, Peter
8 Hall Street
Long Melford
Suffolk CO10 9JG
Sudbury (0787) 880660
Côte d'Azur

Angel Travel
34 High Street
Borough Green, Sevenoaks
Kent TN15 8BJ
Borough Green (0732)
884109
ABTA
Provence and the Côte d'Azur,
Brittany, Paris

Anglo-Italian Tourist Centre
11 Edgbaston Shopping
Centre, Edgbaston
Birmingham B16 8SH
021-452 1188
Tuscany

Arista Holidays
Delta Kappa Travel
18 Grange Road
Crawley Down
West Sussex RH10 4JT
Copthorne (0342) 715491
ABTA, ATOL, AITO
Crete

Astbury Apartments
31 Baker Street
Middlesbrough
Cleveland TS1 2LF
Middlesbrough (0642)
210163
Formentera

Avon Europe
Lower Quinton
Stratford-upon-Avon
Warwickshire CV37 8SG
Stratford-upon-Avon (0789)
720130
Provence, Brittany,
The Dordogne, Costa Brava

BCH Villa France
15 Winchcombe Road
Frampton Cotterell
Bristol
Avon BS17 2AG
Winterbourne (0454) 772410
Côte d'Azur, Brittany,
The Dordogne

Beach Villas
8 Market Passage
Cambridge
Cambridgeshire CB2 3QR
Cambridge (0223) 311113
ABTA, ATOL, AITO
France, Greece, Italy, Portugal,
Spain

La Bella Toscana
Loc. Sovestro-Lignite
53037 San Gimignano
Italy
010-39-577942072
Tuscany

Belvedere Holiday Apartments
5 Bartholomews
Brighton
East Sussex BN1 1HG
Brighton (0273) 23404
Côte d'Azur

Best Travel *see* Grecian Holidays

Bingley & Miller
69a High Street
Littlehampton
West Sussex BN17 5EJ
Littlehampton (0903) 713078
The Algarve

Blakes Holidays
Hoverton Road
Wroxham
Norwich NR12 8DH
Norwich (0603) 784141
Provence, Brittany, The
Dordogne, The Loire, Tuscany,
Costa Brava

Bowhill Holidays
Mayhill Farm, Swanmore
Southampton
Hampshire SO3 2QW
Southampton (0489) 878567
AITO
Provence and the Côte d'Azur,
Brittany, The Dordogne,
The Loire, Tuscany,
The Estoril coast

Bridgewater Villas
37 King Street West
Manchester M3 2PW
061-832 5248
ABTA
Tuscany, Umbria

Bridgeway Travel Services
Emerson House, Heyes Lane
Alderley Edge
Cheshire SK9 7LF
Alderley Edge (0625) 585196
The Algarve

Brimar International
Field House
Wellington Road
Dewsbury
West Yorkshire WF13 1HF
Dewsbury (0924) 454300
Brittany

Brits Abroad
6 Stamford Arcade
Ashton-under-Lyne
Greater Manchester OL6 6JY
061-343 1233
Costa Blanca, Costa del Sol

Brittany Direct Holidays
Cavalier House
362 Sutton Common Road
Sutton, Surrey SM3 9PL
081-641 6060
ABTA, ATOL
Brittany

Brittany Ferries
Millbay Docks
Plymouth
Devon PL1 3EW
Plymouth (0705) 751708
PSA
Brittany, The Dordogne

Burstin Travel
Palace Hotel, Pier Hill
Southend-on-Sea
Essex SS1 3EJ
Southend-on-Sea (0702)
   613011
ABTA, ATOL
*The Algarve, Costa Blanca,
   Costa del Sol, Majorca*

Cabo Roig Villas & Apartments
75 Irby Road, Heswall
Wirral, Cheshire L61 6UY
051-342 6885
Costa Blanca

Cala d'Or Villas
95 Station Road
West Wickham
Kent BR4 0PX
081-777 0025
ATOL
Majorca

Casa Colonica
Suite 8, London House
266 Fulham Road
London SW10 9EL
071-376 4747
Tuscany

Casa International Holidays
3 Elliot Rise, Hedge End
Southampton
Hampshire SO3 4RU
Southampton (0489) 785499
Costa Brava

Castaways
Carew House, Wallington
Surrey SM6 0DG
081-773 2616
ABTA, ATOL, AITO
Majorca

Catalan Villas
Bell Corner
Milverton M10, Taunton
Somerset TA4 1NT
Milverton (0823) 400356
Costa Brava

Celtic Line Travel
94 King Street
Maidstone
Kent ME14 1BH
Maidstone (0622) 690009
ATOL
Minorca

Chalets de France
Travel House, Pandy
Abergavenny
Gwent NP7 8DH
Crucorney (0873) 890770
*Côte d'Azur, Brittany,
   The Dordogne*

Chapter Travel
102 St John's Wood Terrace
London NW8 7ST
071-722 9560
ABTA
*Provence and the Côte d'Azur,
   The Dordogne, Paris, Tuscany,
   Umbria*

Chez Nous
Netherley House
85 Dobb Top Road
Holmbridge, Huddersfield
West Yorkshire HD7 1QP
Holmfirth (0484) 682503
The Dordogne

Citalia
Marco Polo House
3–5 Lansdowne Road
Croydon CR9 1LL
081-686 5533
ABTA, ATOL
Tuscany, Umbria, Venice

City Cruiser Holidays
29–31 Leicester Street
Bedworth
Warwickshire CV12 8JP
Bedworth (0203)
   310033
ABTA
*Adriatic Riviera, Costa Brava,
   Costa Dorada*

Clearwater Holidays
17 Heath Terrace
Leamington Spa
Warwickshire CV32 5NA
Leamington Spa (0926)
   450002
Brittany

Club Cantabrica
Holiday House
146–148 London Road
St Albans
Hertfordshire AL1 1PQ
St Albans (0727) 33141
ABTA, ATOL
*Corfu, Costa Brava, Costa
   Dorada*

Club Pollensa Holidays
13 Montague Place
Worthing
West Sussex BN11 3BG
Worthing (0903) 30128
Majorca

Coast & Country Villas
The Terry Business Centre
Milsbro Road, Redditch
Hereford & Worcester
   B98 7AH
Redditch (0527) 60663
Brittany

Continental Villas
Eagle House
58 Blythe Road
London W14 0HA
071-371 1313
*Côte d'Azur, Tuscany,
   The Algarve, Costa del Sol,
   Majorca, Ibiza*

Cordon Rouge Villas
18–20 Clifton Street
Blackpool
Lancashire FY1 1JP
Blackpool (0253) 25050
Côte d'Azur

Corfu à la Carte
8 Deanwood House
Stockcross, Newbury
Berkshire RG16 8JP
Newbury (0635) 30621
ABTA, ATOL, AITO
Corfu

Cornisa Travel and
   Villas
22 Blenheim Terrace
London NW8 0EB
071-624 8829
ABTA, ATOL
Costa del Sol, The Algarve

Cosmos
Tourama House
17 Holmesdale Road
Bromley, Kent BR2 9LX
081-464 3444
ABTA, ATOL
*Rhodes, The Algarve, The
    Spanish Costas, Majorca,
    Minorca, Ibiza*

Costa Blanca Holiday
Glorieta del Pais
Valencia 6
Apartado 425
E-03700 Denia
Alicante, Spain
010-34-65787579
Costa Blanca

Cresta Holidays
32 Victoria Street
Altrincham
Cheshire WA14 1ET
061-927 7000
ABTA, ATOL
*Provence and the Côte d'Azur,
    Brittany, The Dordogne*

Crockford Enterprises
8 The Magpies
Epping Green, Epping
Essex CM16 6QG
Epping (0378) 78146
The Algarve

Crystal Holiday
The Courtyard
Arlington Road
Surbiton
Surrey KT6 6BW
081-399 5144
ABTA, ATOL
*Côte d'Azur, Brittany,
    The Dordogne, Costa Brava*

CV Travel
43 Cadogan Street
London SW3 2PR
071-581 0851
ABTA, ATOL
*Côte d'Azur, Corfu, Crete,
    Tuscany, The Algarve*

Denia Holidays
PO Box 174, Northampton
Northamptonshire NN3 5BY
Northampton (0604) 784940
Costa Blanca

Destination Portugal
Witney Travel
Madeira House
37 Corn Street, Witney
Oxfordshire OX8 7BW
Witney (0993) 773269
ABTA
The Algarve

Destination Provence
28 rue de la République
83270 St-Cyr-sur-Mer
Var, France
In the UK phone
Watford (0923) 262196
Provence

Dominique's Villas
Park House
140 Battersea Park Road
London SW11 4WB
071-738 8772
*Provence and the Côte d'Azur,
    The Dordogne, The Loire*

Drive Europe
40 Market Place South
Leicester
Leicestershire LE1 5HB
Leicester (0533) 513161
ABTA
Côte d'Azur, Brittany

DSI Services (Nerja)
Deerhurst, Epping Road
Roydon, Harlow
Essex CM19 5RD
Roydon (0279) 792162
Costa del Sol

Enterprise
see Redwing Holidays

ESP Travel & Leisure Services
32 Coronation Road
Mapperley, Nottingham
Nottinghamshire NG3 5JS
Nottingham (0602) 691148
The Algarve

Espan Apartments
178 Crofton Lane
Petts Wood, Orpington
Kent BR6 0BW
Orpington (0689) 20065
Costa del Sol, Majorca

Estartit Owners' Club
Diamond Cottage
Marcia Rice Court
High Street, Abbots Bromley
Staffordshire WS15 3BL
Burton-on-Trent (0283)
   840634
Costa Brava

Euro Express
Apollo House
Church Road
Lowfield Heath, Crawley
West Sussex
Crawley (0293) 511125
ABTA, ATOL, AITO
Côte d'Azur

European Villas
154–156 Victoria Road
Cambridge
Cambridgeshire CB4 3DZ
Cambridge (0223) 314220
ATOL, AITO, ABTA
Provence and the Côte d'Azur,
   Corfu, The Algarve,
   Costa Blanca, Ibiza

Eurovillas
36 East Street
Coggeshall, Colchester
Essex CO6 1SH
Coggeshall (0376) 561156
Côte d'Azur, Brittany,
   The Dordogne, Tuscany

Exclusive Javea Villas
85 Tranby Lane, Anlaby
Hull, Humberside HU10 7DT
Hull (0482) 651890
Costa Blanca

Exclusive Villas
2 Highbury Road
Wimbledon
London SW19 7PR
081-947 7300
Côte d'Azur, The Algarve

Executive Villas
7 Adderley Street
Birmingham B9 4EE
021-766 8410
Costa Blanca

Falcon de-Luxe Resorts
Valentines House
Ilford Hill, Ilford
Essex IG1 2DG
081-514 5555
ABTA, ATOL
The Algarve, Costa del Sol

Falcon Holidays
33 Notting Hill Gate
London W11 3JQ
071-221 6298
ABTA, ATOL
Corfu, Crete, Rhodes

**Fencott Barnes
  International**
227 Maryvale Road
Bourneville
Birmingham B30 2DL
021-779 2313
Costa Blanca

Fidesca Lda
Charneca do Cotifo
Bensafrim, 8600 Lagos
Portugal
010-35-18267181
The Algarve

Fincasol Holidays
4 Bridge Street
Salisbury
Wiltshire SP1 2LX
Salisbury (0722) 411644
Costa del Sol

**Forest Downs
  Investments**
see Ward, Kenneth

Four Seasons
Springfield
Pudsey, Leeds
West Yorkshire LS28 5LY
Leeds (0532) 564374
Brittany

La France des Villages
Model Farm, Rattlesden
Bury St Edmunds
Suffolk 1P30 0SY
Rattlesden (044 93) 7664
Provence

France Directe
2 Church Street
Warwick
Warwickshire CV34 4AB
Warwick (0926) 497989
ABTA
*Provence and the Côte d'Azur,
  Brittany*

France Voyages
145 Oxford Street
London W1R 1TB
071-494 3155
ABTA, ATOL
Brittany

Freelance Holidays
Pound House, Shottery
Stratford-upon-Avon
Warwickshire CV37 9HD
Stratford-upon-Avon (0789)
  297705
Crete, Majorca

French Affair
34 Lillie Road
London SW16 1TW
071-381 8519
The Dordogne

**French Country
  Cottages**
Anglia House
The Marina
Lowestoft
Suffolk NR32 1PZ
Lowestoft (0502) 589171
*Provence, Brittany,
  The Dordogne*

French Life

26 Church Street
Horsforth, Leeds
West Yorkshire LS18 5LG
Leeds (0532) 390077
ABTA
Provence and the Côte d'Azur,
Brittany, The Dordogne,
The Loire

French Travel Service

69 Boston Manor Road
Brentford TW8 9JG
ABTA, ATOL
Côte d'Azur, Paris

French Villa Centre

175 Selsdon Park Road
South Croydon CR2 8JJ
081-651 1231
Provence and the Côte d'Azur,
Brittany, The Dordogne

Geoff Williamson Travel

Chenoya, Calthorpe Road
Fleet, Hampshire GU13 8LN
Fleet (0252) 613325
Majorca

Gîtes de France

178 Piccadilly
London W1V 9DB
071-493 3480
ABTA
Provence and the Côte d'Azur,
Brittany, The Dordogne,
The Loire

Global Air Holidays

North Tower
Bank of America House
26 Elmfield Road
Bromley
Kent BR1 1LR
081-466 4625
ABTA, ATOL
Corfu, Crete, Rhodes, The Algarve,
The Spanish Costas,
The Balearics

GMF Holidays

Graycourt, Old Avenue
West Byfleet
Surrey KT14 6AE
Byfleet (093 23) 55275
Côte d'Azur

Grainger Properties

49 High Street, Chobham
Surrey GU24 8AF
Camberley (0276) 855292
The Algarve

Grecian Holidays

Best Travel
31 Topsfield Parade
Tottenham Lane
London N8 8PT
081-341 7171
ABTA, ATOL
Corfu, Crete, Rhodes

Greco-file

Sourdock Hill
Barkisland, Halifax
West Yorkshire HX4 0AG
Halifax (0422) 375999
Corfu

Hamilton Holidays

23–31 Waring Street
Belfast BT1 2EQ
Belfast (0232) 231265
ABTA, ATOL
Costa del Sol, Majorca

Harry Shaw Holidays
Mill House, Mill Lane
Binley
Coventry CV3 2DW
Coventry (0203) 431077
Côte d'Azur

Hartland Holidays
Brunswick House
91 Brunswick Crescent
London N11 1EE
081-368 4422
ABTA, ATOL
*The Algarve, Costa del Sol,
Majorca, Minorca*

Harvey's à la Carte
Holiday House
2 Monson Road
Tunbridge Wells
Kent TN1 1NN
Tunbridge Wells
   (0892) 36616
ABTA
Brittany

Headwater Holidays
146 London Road
Northwich
Cheshire CW98 5HH
Northwich (0606) 48699
ABTA, ATOL
The Loire

Holmes Travel
42G Barrack Square
Martlesham Heath
Ipswich
Suffolk IP5 7RF
Ipswich (0473) 610666
Costa del Sol

Horizon Holidays
Broadway
Edgbaston Five Ways
Birmingham B15 1BB
021-643 2727
ABTA, ATOL
*Corfu, Crete, Rhodes,
   The Algarve, Costa del Sol,
   Majorca, Minorca, Ibiza*

Hoseasons Holidays Abroad
Sunway House
Lowestoft
Suffolk NR32 3LT
Lowestoft (0502) 500555
ABTA, ATOL
*Côte d'Azur, Brittany,
   The Dordogne, The Loire*

Ilios Island Holidays
18 Market Square
Horsham
West Sussex RH12 1EU
Horsham (0403) 59788
ABTA, ATOL, AITO
Tuscany, Umbria

Images of France
58 Mulberry Way
South Woodford
London E18 1ED
081-530 8458
Provence

Impact Holidays
Devonshire Chambers
10 Devonshire Street
Carlisle
Cumbria CA3 8LP
Carlisle (0228) 45252
ABTA
Adriatic Riviera, Costa Brava

TOUR OPERATORS

Indamar Apartments
Apartado 195
Garrucha, Almeria
Spain
010-34-51478140
Costa de Almeria

Intasun Holidays
Intasun House
Cromwell Avenue
Bromley
Kent BR2 9AQ
081-290 0511
ABTA, ATOL
Greece, Italy, Spain

Interhome
383 Richmond Road
Twickenham TW1 2EF
081-891 1294
Côte d'Azur, Costa Blanca

International Chapters
102 St John's Wood Terrace
London NW8 6PL
071-722 9560
ABTA
Provence, The Dordogne, Paris,
*   Tuscany, Umbria, Rome*

Invitation to Tuscany
PO Box 2, Trinity Court
Park Street
St Peter Port
Guernsey
Guernsey (0481) 27298
Tuscany

Italian Interlude
Lupus Travel Ltd
91 Regent Street
London W1R 7TB
071-494 2031
ABTA
Tuscany, Umbria,
*   Neapolitan Riviera*

Italian Tours
22 Church Rise
London SE23 2UD
081-291 1450
Tuscany, Umbria

Jafa Holidays
Sycamore Farmhouse
Kenton, near Debenham
Stowmarket
Suffolk IP14 6JJ
Debenham (0728) 860088
Brittany

Javea Villas
see Exclusive Javea Villas

Jean Harper Holidays
20 Walton Road
Stockton Heath
Warrington
Cheshire WA4 6NL
Warrington (0925) 64234
ATOL
Costa del Sol, Minorca

Just Italy
Westbury Travel
1 Belmont Road
Bath, Avon BA1 5DZ
Bath (0225) 443133
ABTA, ATOL
Tuscany, Umbria

Kent Travel Service
16 Bellegrove Road
Welling
Kent DA16 3PZ
081-303 6322
ABTA, ATOL
Costa del Sol

Kingsland Holidays
1 Pounds Park, Plymouth
Devon PL3 4QF
Plymouth (0752) 766822
Provence, The Dordogne

Kosmar Villa Holidays
358 Bowes Road
London N11 1AN
081-368 6833
ABTA, ATOL
Corfu, Crete

Lancaster Holidays
North Tower
Bank of America House
26 Elmfield Road, Bromley
Kent BR1 1LR
081-697 8181
*Corfu, Crete, Rhodes, The
    Spanish Costas, Majorca,
    Ibiza, Formentera*

Lanterna Villas
22 Tonbridge Road
Pembury
Kent TN2 4QL
Pembury (0892) 822053
The Algarve

Leisure Villas
21 Palmerston Road
Wimbledon
London SW19 1PG
081-540 5720
ABTA, ATOL
Corfu

Lunigiana Holidays
71 Busbridge Lane.
Godalming
Surrey GU7 1QQ
Godalming (048 68) 21218
Tuscany

Maclaine Holidays
35 Sandford Mill Road
Cheltenham
Gloucestershire GL53 7QH
Cheltenham (0242) 519508
ATOL
The Algarve

The Magic of Italy
Magic of Travel Ltd
227 Shepherds Bush Road
London W6 7AS
081-741 2151
ABTA, ATOL, AITO
*Tuscany, Umbria,
    Neapolitan Riviera*

The Magic of Spain
Magic of Travel Ltd
227 Shepherds Bush Road
London W6 7AS
081-748 7575
ABTA, ATOL, AITO
Costa del Sol, Majorca

Majorca Apartments & Villas
60 Stainbeck Road
Leeds
West Yorkshire LS7 2PW
Leeds (0532) 786862
Majorca

Manos Holidays
Gillingham House
38–44 Gillingham Street
London SW1V 1HU
071-630 1161
ABTA, ATOL, AITO
Corfu, Crete, Rhodes

Marshall Sutton
9 Butcher Road
Beverley
Humberside HU17 7BR
Hull (0482) 882638
ATOL
Minorca

Martyn Holidays
Westleigh House
390 London Road
Isleworth TW7 5AD
081-847 5041
ABTA, ATOL
*Corfu, Crete, The Algarve,
    The Estoril coast, Majorca,
    Minorca, Ibiza*

Medina Holidays
32 Cranbourn Street
London WC2H 7AD
071-836 4995
ABTA, ATOL
Corfu, Crete

Memories Travel
Heath Lodge, Heath Drive
Potters Bar
Hertfordshire EN6 1EH
Potters Bar (0707) 53560
*The Algarve, Costa del Sol,
    Majorca, Ibiza*

Menco
20 Walton Road
Stockton Heath
Warrington
Cheshire WA4 6NL
Warrington (0925) 64234
ATOL
Minorca

Meon Travel
Meon House
College Street
Petersfield
Hampshire GU32 3JN
Petersfield (0730) 61926
ABTA, ATOL, AITO
*France, Greece, Italy, Portugal,
    Spain*

Meridian Tours
12–16 Dering Street
London W1R 9AB
071-493 2777
ABTA, ATOL
Corfu, Crete

Miraleisure
26 Collington Avenue
Bexhill-on-Sea
East Sussex TN39 3QA
Bexhill-on-Sea (0424)
    213464
Côte d'Azur

Miss France Holidays
132 Anson Road
London NW2 6AP
081-452 5901
Provence, The Dordogne

Mojacar Holidays
PO Box 174
Northampton
Northamptonshire NN3 5BY
Northampton (0604) 784940
Costa de Almeria

Mojacar Villas
119 The Promenade
Cheltenham
Gloucestershire GL50 1NW
Cheltenham (0242) 521339
Costa de Almeria

NAT Holidays
47 Grattan Road
Bradford
West Yorkshire BD1 2QF
Bradford (0274) 760011
ABTA, ATOL
*Côte d'Azur, Brittany, The
    Algarve, The Spanish Costas,
    The Balearics*

New Century Holidays
Cathedral House
Wilkes Way, Truro
Cornwall TR1 2UF
Truro (0872) 72367
ABTA, ATOL
Costa de Almeria

Newman, David
PO Box 733
40 Upperton Road
Eastbourne
East Sussex BN21 4AW
Eastbourne (0323) 410347
ABTA
Provence and the Côte d'Azur,
Brittany, The Dordogne,
The Loire, Tuscany

Now Holidays and Travel
Powdene House
32 Pudding Chare
Newcastle Upon Tyne
Tyne & Wear NE1 1UE
091-261 5651
Formentera

NSS Riviera Holidays
199 Marlborough Avenue
Hull, Humberside HU5 3LG
Hull (0482) 42240
Côte d'Azur

Olympic Holidays
Olympic House
30 Cross Street
London N1 2BG
071-704 9236
ABTA
Corfu, Crete, Rhodes

OSL
Horizon Holiday Shop
Broadway
Edgbaston Five Ways
Birmingham B15 1BB
021-632 6282
ABTA, ATOL
Tuscany, The Algarve, Majorca,
Minorca, Ibiza

The Owners' Syndicate
79 Balham Park Road
London SW12 8EB
081-767 7926
The Algarve, Costa del Sol,
Minorca, Ibiza

P & O European Ferries
Channel House
Channel View Road
Dover
Kent CT17 9TJ
Dover (0304) 214422
ABTA, PSA
Provence, Brittany

Palm Luxury Villas
Palm International
Willowdene, Victoria Road
Heaton, Bolton
Greater Manchester BL1 5AT
Bolton (0204) 849029
Provence and the Côte d'Azur,
Costa Brava, The Algarve

Palmer & Parker Holidays
63 Grosvenor Street
London W1X OAJ
071-493 5725
ABTA, ATOL
Côte d'Azur, The Loire, The
Algarve, Costa del Sol

Paloma Holidays
4–6 Farncombe Road
Worthing
West Sussex BN11 2BE
Worthing (0903) 820710
ABTA, ATOL, AITO
*The Algarve, Costa Blanca,
Costa del Sol, Minorca*

Pan World Holidays
8 Great Chapel Street
London W1V 3AG
071-287 9642
ATOL
Corfu, Crete, Rhodes

Panorama Holiday Group
29 Queens Road
Brighton
East Sussex BN1 3YN
Brighton (0273) 206531
ABTA, ATOL, AITO
Costa Brava, Ibiza

Paramount Holidays
241 King's Road
London SW3 5EL
071-351 3135
Costa del Sol

Patricia Wildblood
Calne
Wiltshire SN11 0LP
Calne (0249) 817023
ABTA, ATOL
Tuscany, The Algarve, Minorca

PDO Holidays
Malton House
24 Hampshire Terrace
Portsmouth
Hampshire PO1 2QE
Portsmouth (0705) 755715
Brittany

Pegasus Holidays
River House
Restmor Way
Hackbridge Road
Wallington
Sutton SM6 7AH
081-773 2323
ABTA, ATOL
*Tuscany, Umbria, Neapolitan
Riviera*

Perrymead Properties
55 Perrymead Street
London SW6 3SN
071-736 4592
Tuscany

Pleasurewood Holidays
see French Country Cottages

Portugal Connections
29 South Street
Chichester
West Sussex PO19 1EL
Chichester (0243) 776211
ABTA
The Algarve

The Portuguese Property Bureau
Algarve House
The Colonnade
Maidenhead
Berkshire SL6 1QL
Maidenhead (0628) 32788
ABTA, ATOL
The Algarve

Premier Property Services
7 Greenview Drive
Towcester
Northamptonshire NN12 7BL
Towcester (0327) 50394
Costa Blanca

La Première Quality Villas

Cerbid, Solva
Haverfordwest
Dyfed SA62 6YE
Croesgoch (0348) 837871
Provence and the Côte d'Azur,
   Brittany

Prime Time Holidays

Iroko House
Station Road
Derby
Derbyshire
Derby (0332) 291503
ABTA
Brittany, The Dordogne

Les Propriétaires de l'Ouest

Malton House
24 Hampshire Terrace
Southsea
Hampshire PO1 2QE
Portsmouth (0705) 755715
Provence, Brittany,
   The Dordogne

Pure Crete

Acorn House
74 Cherry Orchard Road
Croydon CR0 6BA
081-760 0879
Crete

Purely Portugal

178a Harefield Road
Uxbridge UB8 1PP
Uxbridge (0895) 36972
The Algarve, The Estoril coast

Quo Vadis

243 Euston Road
London NW1 2BT
071-387 6122
ABTA, ATOL
Côte d'Azur

R & R Travel Services

1 Charlesville Place
Neath
West Glamorgan SA11 1PY
Neath (0639) 645603
Costa Blanca, Costa del Sol,
   Majorca, Ibiza

Realcare Villa Services

4 Bordesley Court
Lillington Road
Leamington Spa
Warwickshire CV32 6NR
Leamington Spa (0926)
   316138
Minorca

Redwing Holidays

Groundstar House
London Road
Crawley
West Sussex RH10 2DB
Crawley (0293) 561999
ABTA, ATOL
Some self-catering in
   Enterprise, Sovereign and
   Sunmed programmes.

Rendezvous France

Holiday House
19 Aylesbury Road
Wendover
Buckinghamshire HP22 6JG
Aylesbury (0296) 696040
ABTA
Provence and the Côte d'Azur,
   Brittany, The Dordogne,
   The Loire

Rentavilla

27 High Street
Chesterton
Cambridge
Cambridgeshire CB4 1ND
Cambridge (0223) 323414
ABTA, ATOL
France, Greece, Portugal, Spain

Roc Villas
44 Brockbridge House
Tangley Grove
Roehampton
London SW15 4EN
081-878 1205
Costa del Sol

Saga Holidays
The Saga Building
Middleburg Square
Folkestone
Kent CT20 1AZ
0800-300 500
ABTA, ATOL
Côte d'Azur, The Algarve,
   Costa Blanca, Costa de
   Almeria, Majorca

Sally Holidays
81 Piccadilly
London W1V 9HF
071-355 2266
PSA
Côte d'Azur, The Dordogne

San Clemente Villas
Sa Vinya
29 Avenida del Dr Guardia
Mahon, Minorca, Spain
010-34-71360434
Minorca

Savoir-Faire
69 rue Général de Gaulle
56300 Pontivy, France
010-33-97278610
Brittany

SBH France
Cavalier House
Tangmere, Chichester
West Sussex PO20 6HE
Chichester (0243) 773345
Brittany, The Dordogne,
   The Loire

Sealink Holidays
Charter House
Park Street
Ashford
Kent TN24 8EX
Ashford (0233) 647033
ABTA, PSA
Côte d'Azur, Brittany,
   The Dordogne, The Loire,
   Costa Brava

Seasun Tentrek
71–72 East Hill
Colchester
Essex CO1 2QW
Colchester (0206) 869888
ABTA, ATOL
Adriatic Riviera, The Algarve,
   Costa Brava

Secker, Catherine
102a Burnt Ash Lane
Bromley
Kent BR1 4DD
081-460 8022
Crete

Select Holidays
Centurion House
Bircherley Street
Hertford
Hertfordshire SG14 1BH
Hertford (0992) 554144
The Algarve, Costa del Sol,
   Majorca

SFV Holidays
Summer House, Hermes Road
Summertown
Oxford
Oxfordshire OX2 7PU
Oxford (0865) 311331
ATOL
Provence and the Côte d'Azur,
   Brittany, Tuscany, Costa
   Brava, Costa Blanca

Simply Crete
8 Chiswick Terrace
Acton Lane
London W4 5LY
081-994 4462
ATOL, AITO
Crete

Skytours
Greater London House
Hampstead Road
London NW1 7SD
071-387 9321
ABTA, ATOL
Corfu, Crete

Slipaway Holidays
90 Newland Road
Worthing
West Sussex BN11 1LB
Worthing (0903) 821000
*Côte d'Azur, Brittany,
    The Dordogne, The Loire*

**Something Special
    Travel**
10 Bull Plain
Hertford
Hertfordshire SG14 1DT
Hertford (0992) 552231
ABTA, ATOL, AITO
*Corfu, The Algarve, Costa
    Blanca, Majorca*

**Southern Brittany
    Holidays**
see SBH France

Sovereign
see Redwing Holidays

**Spanish Harbour
    Holidays**
The Cottage, Upper Street
Dyrham, Chippenham
Wiltshire SN14 8HW
Abson (0275) 823759
Costa Brava

Starvillas
25 High Street
Chesterton
Cambridge
Cambridgeshire CB4 1ND
Cambridge (0223) 311990
ATOL
France, Greece, Portugal, Spain

Sturge, Martin
3 Lower Camden Place
Bath
Avon BA1 5JJ
Bath (0225) 310623
The Dordogne

Sunmed
see Redwing Holidays

Sunscene Holidays
40 Market Place South
Leicester
Leicestershire LE1 5HB
Leicester (0533) 620644
ABTA
*Côte d'Azur, Costa Brava,
    Costa Dorada*

Sunseekers
Revenue Chambers
St Peter's Street
Huddersfield
West Yorkshire HO1 1DL
Huddersfield (0484) 511224
ABTA, ATOL
Crete

TOUR OPERATORS

Sunselect Villas
60 Crow Hill North
Middleton
Manchester M24 1FB
061-655 3055
Brittany

Sunset Villas
White Cottage
off Grange Lane
Rushwick
Worcester
Hereford & Worcester
WR2 5TG
Worcester (0905) 422775
Costa Blanca

Sunvil Travel
Sunvil House
7–8 Upper Square
Old Isleworth TW7 7BJ
081-568 4499
ABTA, ATOL, AITO
Corfu, Crete

Sunvista Holidays
5a George Street
Warminster
Wiltshire BA12 8QA
Warminster (0985) 214666
ABTA, AITO
*Côte d'Azur, Brittany,
The Dordogne, The Loire*

Sunwest Travel
25 St Mary's Street
Thornbury, Bristol
Avon BS12 2AQ
Thornbury (0454) 418888
Costa del Sol

Tarleton Travel
Tarleton House
16 Uttoxeter Road, Tean
Stoke-on-Trent
Staffordshire ST10 4LG
Tean (0538) 722231
ATOL
Costa de Almeria

Thomson Holidays
Greater London House
Hampstead Road
London NW1 7SD
071-387 9321
ABTA, ATOL
*Corfu, Crete, The Algarve,
Costa Blanca, Majorca,
Minorca, Ibiza*

Timsway Holidays
see Tjaerborg

Tjaerborg
194 Campden Hill Road
London W8 7TH
071-727 2680
ATOL
*Corfu, Crete, The Algarve, The
Spanish Costas, The Balearics*

Traditional Tuscany
208 Westcombe Park Road
Blackheath
London SE3 7RZ
081-305 1380
Tuscany

The Travel Club
Station Road
Upminster
Essex RM14 2TT
Upminster (040 22) 25000
ABTA, ATOL
Crete, The Algarve